The Pursuit
of Wilderness

The Pursuit
of Wilderness

PAUL BROOKS

with photographs and maps

Houghton Mifflin Company, Boston

1971

MAPS BY SAMUEL H. BRYANT

First printing   w

At the same time that we are earnest to explore and learn all things, we require that all things be mysterious and unexplorable, that land and sea be infinitely wild, unsurveyed and unfathomed by us because unfathomable. We can never have enough of nature. We must be refreshed by the sight of inexhaustible vigor, vast and titanic features, the sea-coast with its wrecks, the wilderness with its living and its decaying trees, the thunder-cloud, and the rain which lasts three weeks and produces freshets. We need to witness our own limits transgressed, and some life pasturing freely where we never wander.

HENRY DAVID THOREAU, *Walden*

Acknowledgments

M OST OF THE MATERIAL in this book has appeared, in slightly different form, in the *Atlantic, Harper's, Horizon, Audubon, Sierra Club Bulletin,* and the *New York Times.* Permission to use it here is gratefully acknowledged.

The account of Project Chariot in Chapter 4 was originally written in collaboration with Joseph Foote, then on the staff of the *Providence Journal.* His contribution is deeply appreciated.

Anyone who writes about such diverse areas and conservation issues is necessarily indebted to those persons working in the field who have far more knowledge of the local situation than he can ever hope to achieve. I trust that many friends who have helped me in gathering facts presented here will forgive what may often seem an oversimplification of a complex and ever-changing story.

Finally, I wish to express my appreciation to Helen Phillips and Katharine Bernard for the care and imagination that they brought to the editing and production of this book.

Photographs

THE PHOTOGRAPHS in this book come from many sources, too numerous to list here. Those depicting the Northwest and Alaska are principally by Philip Hyde, who has traveled much in the Cascades and was a member of our group on the Yukon. For the birds and other wildlife of Florida, I am indebted to Frederick Kent Truslow, dean of American bird photographers. Since the subjects are largely self-explanatory, and the pictures complement rather than specifically illustrate the narrative, captions have been omitted; identifications and credits will be found on pages 217–219.

Contents

Maps

Preface

WE ARE TODAY engaged in a Second American Revolution: not this time against oppression from abroad, but against conditions that we have ourselves created at home. It may not be recognized as a revolution because it started many years ago, and quietly, in the sense that few voices were raised and few people listened. It has gathered momentum slowly and it has operated within the law. The battles, though often dramatic and bitter, have been largely legal and political, thus making them difficult for the layman to follow. Now suddenly conservation is "in." With the advent of the population scare, it has even replaced motherhood as the safest of all things to be for. What has happened?

Neither a fad nor a cult, this bloodless revolt springs from a new understanding of man's place in nature. It is based on the simple premise that concern for the environment — including our remaining wilderness — is no less fundamental than concern for economic prosperity, or for political and human rights. Such thinking, however, is comparatively recent. Revolutions seldom occur until pressures make them inevitable.

Owing to the sheer size and fertility of our continent, we in America are only now reaching the point where the pressures on our environment are greater than it can tolerate.

Central to the modern conservation movement is the principle that a citizen has a legitimate interest in the environment as a whole, not merely in the piece of real estate to which he happens to hold title. This is a revolutionary doctrine, if one interprets the so-called "free enterprise system" to mean freedom to exploit one's property at whatever cost to others. But actually it represents a return to an earlier ideal: an ideal underscored by that significant change in the original wording of the Declaration of Independence, from "Life, Liberty, and Property" to "Life, Liberty, and the Pursuit of Happiness." Young Americans in particular reject the assumption that the gross national product is the measure of the good life — as if exploitation of nature were synonymous with success. Everywhere there is springing up a new "land ethic," a respect for the land itself, independent of any monetary use to which it may be put. This attitude finds its purest expression in the value we attach to our remaining unspoiled wilderness.

While wilderness represents the essence of quiet and serenity, its defenders are necessarily voluble and noisy. As one listens to their speeches and reads their writings, one is reminded of the contemporary quip about Thomas Carlyle that he preached the doctrine of silence in forty volumes. Alas, this noise (to which I am now contributing) must get ever louder as our wilderness disappears at an ever faster rate. In the shadow of a needless and destructive dam, for example, built as a boondoggle by the Army Engineers, one cannot ignore the old Hungarian maxim: "If you are among the brigands and you are silent, you are a brigand yourself."

In this book I have described certain key battles for wilderness, all but one of which has reached its climax during the past five years. I have confined myself to areas about which I have some personal knowledge, and made no attempt to cover the wilderness front as a whole. (I have not, for example, described two of the most publicized battles of recent years, those to prevent the damming of the Grand Canyon and to establish an adequate Redwoods National Park). Following a brief analysis of some key words in the conservationist's vocabulary, I have touched on three parts of North America where wilderness is both spectacular and in more than usual danger from outside pressures: the Northwest, Alaska, and Florida; and two other world conservation issues: the fate of the great game herds of East Africa, and the preservation of that living symbol of wildness, the rhinoceros — whose very existence is threatened by a superstition inherited from the Dark Ages. In each case I have included an account of a personal wilderness experience as a small sample of what we are fighting for.

Most of the issues I deal with are, unfortunately, still very much alive. By the nature of their cause, defenders of our wilderness can never lay down their arms. They are fighting against unequal odds, since what they lose is lost forever, while what they win must generally be fought for another day.

I F ALL THE LIPS that serve conservationists were laid end-to-end, there would be a lot of fixed smiles," wrote a disillusioned conservationist a few years ago. "For in spite of the seriousness of our environmental problems, the conservation effort still consists largely of words." The fact is, of course, that any action — at least in a democratic society — starts with words. It may be a flood of words from a multitude of sources, as is represented by the seemingly endless hearings required for any federal legislation. It may be a book like *Deserts on the March* by Paul Sears, *Sand County Almanac* by Aldo Leopold, *Road to Survival* by William Vogt, or *Silent Spring* by Rachel Carson, where eloquent words, backed by irrefutable scientific fact, have been used to shock us into realization of what we are doing to our environment. It may be a short magazine article. The evidence shows that words *are* effective. Even the most monolithic power structures are sensitive to public opinion — indeed one sometimes feels that this is the only thing they are sensitive to. Conservationists need words because what they are trying to do is to enlighten and inform: to change fundamental attitudes, not because they say so, but because they have the facts that will command such change on the part of any reasonable man. Their objective is to bridge the gap between an informed minority (I refer specifically to conservation issues) and an uninformed majority. The people they are trying to reach — the people whose voices count when it comes to a showdown — are neither ignorant nor thoughtless but, on the contrary, intelligent and generally well-informed people who happen to be uninformed in this area, who have never thought about these matters one way or the other.

During the war when I was with the Office of War Information in Europe, the government had a slogan, "Words are bullets." To anyone who has been exposed to the language known as "Washingtonese" or "governmentese," a Washington bureau seems a strange source for such a metaphor; at the least, the slogan-writer might have used the analogy of a sawed-off shotgun loaded with birdshot. But how well off is the conservation movement itself when it comes to using words as bullets? It suffers, I think, from a severe handicap: scarcely one of its key words has been defined with precision. Some of them have mutually exclusive connotations, depending on the background of the person being addressed. In short, there is no accepted vocabulary to express a set of values which need to be presented precisely and persuasively. This is particularly serious because these values are often in fundamental contradiction to the cherished clichés of the society in which we live.

What are the key words? A few of the commonest are "wilderness," "national park," "recreation," "conservation," "natural environment." The word "wilderness" has been defined quite eloquently in the Wilderness Act as "an area where the earth and its community of life are untrammeled by man, where man himself is a visitor who does not remain." Yet "wilderness" remains literally one of the most ambivalent words in the language: it has two contradictory meanings representing two diametrically opposed values. The biblical meaning of wilderness, which was brought to America by our Puritan forebears, was "desert." It was a hostile environment, a last refuge for outcasts, the place into which you drove the scapegoat laden with the sins of mankind. It could be made to bloom only through man's toil. In that song familiar to some of us in the Boston area, "Fair Harvard," the college is described as the "first flower of our wilderness." It was not a wildflower, you may be sure, that the writer had in mind. He was thinking of a cultivated spot in a surrounding desert. So deeply ingrained was this concept, that heavily forested country continued to be referred to as "desert" — going back to the original meaning of simply an unoccupied area. Wilderness was unholy ground inhabited largely by devils; noisy devils, apparently, since the stock phrase was "howling wilderness." Presumably a "wilderness conference" in those days would have been a sort of witches' sabbath.

To the frontiersman the wilderness was of course an adversary. Only after it had been largely subdued could the surviving fragments be enjoyed. Not till the period of the Romantic Movement in European literature, till the time of Thoreau and the transcendentalists in America, did the term itself become generally respectable. As recently as the 1920s, when the first wilderness areas were established by the Forest

Service, there was serious question as to whether the word "wilderness" would have unfortunate repercussions. Now it has gone to the other extreme and we hear about the "wilderness mystique" and the "wilderness cult." Yet the word continues to be used in a pejorative sense. For example, in a speech about the dangers of pollution, President Johnson warned that our countryside might become "a wilderness of ghost towns." Some modern uses of the term are very odd indeed. A ballet put on in New York was entitled "Wilderness." According to the review in the *New York Times,* it "was clearly about a beautiful girl, a man with leprosy and a slave driver" — the relation between the three of them being somewhat confused. This sort of thing may be covered by the Mann Act, but certainly not by the Wilderness Act.

So what? Does this confusion matter? I believe it does. After all, we think in terms of words, and centuries of folklore and prejudice cannot be changed overnight. To take a parallel example, would the senseless poisoning and shooting of wolves be tolerated by the public if wolves were not still associated with evil? Wilderness, though no longer considered unholy, is still identified in many people's minds with land that is good for nothing else, with wasteland. Mining, lumbering, and grazing interests of course take this view. The Forest Service is occasionally guilty of such thinking. I trust that the National Park Service is not, though I feel sure that in some people's minds the wilderness areas of our parks are those portions not suitable for recreational development. And it is a curious fact that the White House Conference on National Beauty gave scarcely any consideration to the most natural and beautiful areas of all, the wilderness areas.

Unlike the word "wilderness," the term "national park" is less than a hundred years old. It does not carry with it the accumulated prejudice of centuries. Its connotations, except to such special groups as the timber and mining industries, are entirely pleasant. Yet the confusion in the meaning of the term is almost as great as in the case of wilderness; from the point of view of practical politics and administration it may be even more serious. Let me illustrate. Several years ago I was privileged to take part in an international conservation conference in Bangkok, one session of which was devoted to "national parks." We quickly realized that the American delegates understood one thing by this phrase and the Thai delegates (with one notable exception) quite another. To the latter, a park was primarily a place for rural recreation — a sort of national country club. Administration was under the national tourist bureau. The first thing to do was to improve the roads, landscape the area, plant flower beds, build a restaurant and a bar and a golf course. Naturally enough. To them the term "wilderness park" would have been a contradiction in terms.

Nor is this semantic difficulty confined to the so-called "developing countries" in which the national park concept comes as a new idea. In England, for example, a national park is defined in the booklet of the Nature Conservancy as "a thinly inhabited region where the natural scenery is safeguarded for amenity and recreation." To us in America "national park" suggests something very different. But exactly what does it mean?

The word "park" has meant many things to many people. The history of such a word is the history of a concept, and its meanings grow and proliferate over the years. The more widely a concept is approved, the more likely the word itself is to be debased. "Home" and "park" are such words. The "split-level home" and the "funeral home" have now been joined by the "industrial park" that sustains the one and the "memorial park" that sustains the other. Yet if the word "park," like the word "home," didn't stand for something we believe in, there would be no cash value in exploiting it. It does, in fact, denote two different ideas, each admirable in itself but each in conflict with the other. The fact that we have only one word for both is the source of much agony and confusion.

"Park" comes from the old English "parrock" or "paddock" — an enclosed space of ground. In English law it originally referred to lands held by royal grant, principally as hunting reserves. It also applied to the large ornamental grounds of a country estate. By the late seventeenth century, the term was being used to describe open landscaped areas within or near cities set aside for public recreation. But not until recent times was it applied to tracts of wilderness saved by government action from private exploitation. The revolutionary idea of the national park was born in America, about a hundred years ago. The concept was new, and the old word had to be stretched to fit it. As a matter of fact, it stretched rather slowly, since the first parks were established for the sake of their "natural curiosities," rather than to save wilderness as such. Wilderness preservation was at first a by-product of the national parks movement. Today it has become a principal objective. But is the public at large aware of the change?

More and more people are swarming to our national parks.

What do they expect to find when they get there? What do they expect to *do* there?

This leads us to another key word in the conservationist's vocabulary, the word "recreation." The term is so broad as almost to defy definition. It was a lovely word to begin with, meaning "re-creation," creating anew. Today it suggests anything you do when you are not working, including, according to the advertisements for retirement funds, sleeping in a hammock in Florida with a newspaper over your face. If we narrow the question down to recreation in the national parks, we can be a bit more precise. One criterion would be that the activity, whatever it is, should not alter the natural landscape. Another is that it shouldn't hog the environment for itself. For instance, speedboats and water-skiing can drive out canoes, but not vice versa. If we want to talk in the language of the businessman, we can evaluate recreation in terms of consumption. The parks provide a limited space for the use of an increasing number of people. A man in an automobile consumes space many times faster than a man on foot. A speedboat at thirty miles an hour consumes ten times as much space as a canoe at three miles an hour for the same number of hours of recreation.

If we can't define recreation, we can at least make clear what we mean by it in the context of national parks and wilderness areas. We may even claim that the forms of recreation involving outdoor skills, scientific knowledge, artistic appreciation, and one's own muscles — as opposed to those depending on secondhand entertainment or the internal combustion engine — come closest to the original essence of this much watered-down word.

To the uninitiated, much of the official government jargon is also misleading. When the man on the street sees the words "national forest" on a map, he assumes that the area is covered with trees. When he sees the words "national monument," he has every right to visualize a granite obelisk or a bronze statue of a general on horseback. Least of all can we expect him to appreciate the technical distinctions between "roadless area," "primitive area," and "wilderness area." He is, to use a fine old English word, "jargogled."

Next we come face to face with that all-inclusive word that takes in everything we have been talking about: the word "conservation." Today it is an O.K. word. As Sir Frank Fraser Darling has written, "the idea of conservation is easy and emotionally satisfying." This is true, and it can be a source of weakness rather than of strength. To some of our corporation executives, for example, conservation is a nice hobby for old ladies in tennis shoes but it must not be allowed to interfere with the practical business of the country, which, as Calvin Coolidge once reminded us, is business.

The word "conservation" inevitably suggests the word "conservative." It has a negative connotation, as if our only object was preservation of the status quo. We know otherwise. It is a positive concept. And though the idea of conservation may be easy, the practice of conservation, as we have all learned, is very difficult indeed.

We face an obvious dilemma. Ours is a monetary society, based on private enterprise and financial profits. But the values of the wilderness conservation movement cannot be expressed in terms of dollars. Thus for many people they do not exist. This gives an overwhelming advantage to the exploiter. The battle between two standards of values has of course been going on at least since the turn of the century. Yet one is continually struck with the endurance of the old standards. During the fight to save Hetch Hetchy, the conservationists were described as "hoggish and mushy esthetes." Today's strip miner calls them "bleeding hearts and do-gooders who don't understand the real issues." For him, the best coal is the cheapest coal no matter what its exploitation may do to the landscape. To adopt any other criterion would be to violate "the good old American free enterprise system." In his book, "conservation" is simply a dirty word.

Finally, all the words we have been discussing are related to that broad and scarcely definable term, the "natural environment." I shall not try to define it, but I should like to comment on it. We shall never understand the natural environment until we see it not as just so much air, water, and real estate, but as a living organism. Land can be healthy or sick, fertile or barren, rich or poor, lovingly nurtured or bled white. Our present attitudes and laws governing the ownership and use of land represent an abuse of the concept of private property. Land is treated like a commodity when it is in fact a trust. Not so long ago our society permitted one human being to own another — to exploit him and even work him to death and not go to jail for it. This is no longer considered acceptable behavior, either by society or by the law. Yet in America today you can murder land for private profit, as is being done, for example, on a vast scale in the southern Appalachians. You can leave the corpse for all to see, and nobody calls the cops. This situation is what is known in history as a "cultural lag." It has occurred because our understanding has not caught up with our technology: a familiar complaint that has become almost a cliché in reference to dramatic modern inventions like the atomic bomb. It is equally true in respect to less spectacular forms of destruction. You can kill land by skinning it alive or by slowly poisoning it, and it is murder all the same. In the modern world, no one should have life and death control over his land any more than he does over another human being.

— 2 —

The Fight for
America's Alps

I N SEPTEMBER 1968 the United States Congress passed a bill creating a North Cascades National Park. Thus ended one round in the classic contest between those ancient rivals within the American bureaucracy: the U.S. Forest Service (in the Department of Agriculture) and the National Park Service (in the Department of the Interior). Imagine, if you can, Hector and Achilles agreeing on a bipartisan committee to decide the future status of the plains of windy Troy. This will give you some idea of the historic precedent that was set when the Secretaries of Agriculture and Interior appointed in 1963 a five-man study team to produce a plan for the state of Washington's North Cascades. Often referred to as the American Alps, the Cascades are the wildest, most rugged, and probably most beautiful mountains in the United States south of Alaska. They are also the least known. Until recently their inaccessibility has been their salvation. That time is past.

The report of the study team, submitted in 1966, did not mark the end of the battle; on the contrary, it seemed at the time more like the beginning. The North Cascades were under control of the Forest Service, which had the support of the timber, mining, and local hunting interests. The Park Service's bid for a new park in the area was backed by most of the national conservation organizations. But actually the struggle was both deeper and broader than the conventional conflict between these two bureaucracies. It was part of a much larger conservation battle which is being waged, with various degrees of intensity, from Florida to Alaska, from California's Point Reyes to the banks of the Hudson River. Among the giant redwoods, in the depths of the Grand Canyon, on the north slope of the Brooks Range, organized nature lovers are testing their political strength. The bird-watchers, the photographers, the campers and the climbers are making themselves heard above the chain saws and the bulldozers. They are no longer to be shrugged off by the corporate executive and the political "realist" as a lunatic fringe. They have become organized, sophisticated, articulate. The intangible values they stand for have caught the attention of the giant foundations which are concerned with the future pattern of the good society. They have even been given legal standing by the courts. Congressmen who want to be re-elected are forced to listen. Indeed, Congress itself officially recognized the existence of wilderness, when it passed the Wilderness Act in 1964, and the White House under President Johnson went down the line for "natural beauty." Everywhere the conservation issue has become politically hot. When the chairman of the North Cascades study team, Edward C. Crafts, director of the Bureau of Outdoor Recreation, submitted his report, he was quite explicit: "I know of nothing that I have been involved in in my 32 years' experience that has been more controversial up to this point and I think the controversy is probably only beginning."

Secretary of Agriculture Orville L. Freeman called the North Cascades "one of the most magnificent areas in the world." Two visits to these mountains, including a fortnight's family pack trip in the summer of 1966, convinced me that he was right, and that there was an opportunity here for the most beautiful wilderness park in our entire national park system. Yet the eventual fate of the North Cascades concerned more than this area alone. In a stage setting worthy of the issues at stake, we were watching the confrontation of rock-bottom conservation philosophies, involving basic principles as well as power politics. Here in one of the last unopened corners of our country we faced the ultimate questions: What future do we want for the remnant of wild America, and to whom shall we entrust it?

The Cascade Range, which runs from northern California north across Oregon and Washington to southern Canada, is actually two mountain systems: the famous volcanic cones like Mount Hood, Mount St. Helens, Mount Rainier, Mount Baker; and the far less familiar mass of granite and metamorphic rock peaks between Seattle and the Canadian border. The name "Cascades" derives from the Great Falls of the Columbia, the supreme challenge faced by Lewis and Clark on their historic journey to the Pacific. "This Chanel [they wrote in their journal for October 25, 1805] is through a hard rough black rock, from 50 to 100 yards wide, swelling and boiling in a most tremendious maner." The Columbia's cascades have now been drowned by Bonneville Dam, but

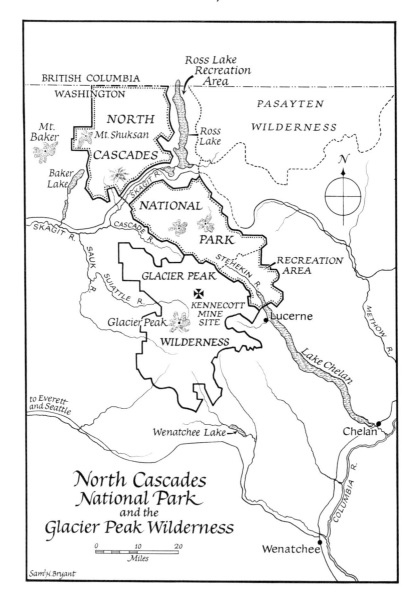

Ross Lake
Recreation
Area

BRITISH COLUMBIA
WASHINGTON

PASAYTEN

WILDERNESS

NORTH

Mt.
Baker
Mt. Shuksan
Ross
Lake

CASCADES

Baker
Lake

SKAGIT R.

NATIONAL

SKAGIT R.
CASCADE R.

PARK

SAUK R.
SUIATTLE R.

GLACIER PEAK

STEHEKIN R.

RECREATION
AREA

KENNECOTT
MINE
SITE

Glacier Peak

Lucerne

METHOW R.

WILDERNESS

Lake Chelan

to Everett
and Seattle

COLUMBIA R.

Wenatchee Lake

Chelan

North Cascades
National Park
and the
Glacier Peak Wilderness

0   10   20
Miles

Wenatchee

Sam¹H.Bryant

the name is still appropriate to these glacier-clad mountains, where the sound of roaring streams is a constant companion on the forest trails and where innumerable ribbons of bright water lace the steep valley walls.

The Cascades are "new" mountains, not yet worn down by erosion; their pinnacles and knife-sharp ridges are still being chiseled by the ice. Of moderate height, from 8000 to 10,000 feet, they seem much higher as they rise sheer from deep valleys near sea level. The classic eastern approach is by boat up fjordlike Lake Chelan. This spectacular body of water, 1500 feet deep (the bottom is below sea level), was formed during the Ice Age by the glacial gouging of a valley subsequently dammed by a moraine. For fifty-five miles it cuts a way into the heart of the North Cascades. Little wonder that as early as 1906 (ten years before the founding of the National Park Service) a mountaineering group urged that Lake Chelan and the surrounding mountains be made a national park. Thirty years later, a committee of the Park Service itself reported that "the area is unquestionably of national park caliber, is more valuable used as such than for any other use now ascertainable." Why, then, wasn't a North Cascades National Park created years ago? The answer lies in the tangled history of our public domain.

Without some knowledge of what has gone before, the struggle for the American wilderness, including the Park Service–Forest Service feud, is as incomprehensible to the average sane American as *Who's Afraid of Virginia Woolf?* would be to the average sane Eskimo. A hundred years ago the American forest was being plundered on a scale we now find inconceivable. Millions of acres were acquired by the

railroads and timber interests through political chicanery and outright fraud. The slogan was "cut and get out." The first effective opposition to this looting arose in the 1860s and 1870s, when the park idea took hold under the leadership of men like John Muir and Frederick Law Olmsted. In the late eighties the federal government established a Division of Forestry in the Department of Agriculture. Shortly afterward, the forest reserves (later called national forests) were set up under the Department of Interior. This was the situation when Theodore Roosevelt succeeded to the Presidency. One of his first acts was to urge Congress to transfer the forest reserves to the Bureau of Forestry in the Department of Agriculture, "to which they properly belong. The present diffusion of responsibility is bad from every standpoint." Roosevelt was further influenced by the fact that his trusted friend Gifford Pinchot, a man of integrity, with courage to fight the lumber barons, was head of the Bureau of Forestry (later to be renamed the U.S. Forest Service). The Transfer Act was quickly passed. T.R. and Pinchot went on to set aside 132 million acres of forest reserves — land to be used, but only under government supervision. Large-scale conservation had been born.

Thus matters stood in 1916 when, despite opposition by the Forest Service, the National Park Service was established in the Department of the Interior. Its purpose was to administer the national parks, monuments, and Indian reservations already in existence (beginning with Yellowstone in 1872), to keep them "unimpaired for the enjoyment of future generations," and inevitably to recommend additions to the park system as need arose. Since most of the available areas of national park caliber were (and are) in the national forests, new parks must be carved out of the Forest Service empire, and thus transferred from Agriculture to Interior. Each such attempt has been a casus belli. But never was the "territorial imperative," as the old instinct is now fashionably called, more nakedly displayed than in the Forest Service's opposition to a national park in the North Cascades. In the case of the baboon, ethologists tell us, the mere baring of the huge canine teeth is generally enough to make the invader retreat. The situation here was perhaps more subtle, and the conditions of the jungle made behavioral studies much more difficult.

The Cascades fight, however, clarified one essential point: the character of the contest (aside from mere possession of territory) has changed in the last fifty years, as America has changed. Great conservationist though he was, Gifford Pinchot was curiously blind to any "use" of our forests beyond the purely utilitarian; the preservation of wilderness for its aesthetic or spiritual qualities was not his concern. Since his time, the Service that he founded to control the lumber interests has become more and more their spokesman. Yet by the time of the Cascades controversy, the Forest Service had been forced to recognize that recreation is a valid forest product which is, moreover, getting the political support that government empires live and grow on. Meanwhile, the Park Service had seized for its own the popular slogan of recreation. Under that banner it had been carrying out "improvements" elsewhere in its domain that made its most loyal supporters uneasy about its plans for the North Cascades.

· ·

These were some of the questions and confusions that I carried with me when my family and I set out in August 1966 for our two-week camping trip, by horse and pack mule, into the "American Alps." This time we entered not by way of Lake Chelan, as we had four years earlier, but by Washington Pass at the northeastern edge of the range. It was a sudden, dramatic entry compared with the leisurely journey up the lake; in a matter of minutes we were surrounded by sharp rock peaks, with glimpses of high snowfields beyond. To the wilderness lover it was also jarring. Here was the beginning of a cross-mountain road, the first to be cut through this hitherto roadless area. There is something almost obscene in the power of modern technology to subdue the landscape; no slope is so steep, no rock is so hard but it yields at last. Not till we had turned off the main trail, with its ominous surveyors' ribbons, and climbed up to a high mountain tarn did we sense that lifting of the spirit that comes on entering the true wilderness.

On the gentle incline below the lake itself, enough soil has built up over the centuries to nourish grass, low shrubs, and a variety of wildflowers that make a mass of color visible even at a distance. Only the meadow near the outlet is level enough for a tent. Here a tiny stream winds along the valley floor. Fallen trees and debris have dammed it every few hundred yards along its course, creating a chain of shallow grass-margined ponds, at first glance almost like the work of beavers. The turf is moist and heavy, bright with red splashes of monkey-flower, thick clumps of blue northern gentian, and the delicate white western anemone.

A lake in such a setting almost compels the term "American

Alps." It lies, green-blue and crystal clear, at the bottom of
a cup in the mountains. Steep talus slopes, mottled with dark
clumps of alpine fir and bright patches of snow, rise straight

from the water's edge, evidence that the lake is deep as well as cold. Far up the mountain a marmot whistles, and another answers. From the foot of a rockslide comes the strange little squeak of a "rock rabbit." The pika, as he is properly called, is shy but curious. Wait a moment in silence, and he will emerge into clear view to look you over.

The full beauty of a mountain lake, however, can be realized only from above. Next morning when the early fog had blown out of the valley, we set out on foot up the trail to the pass. Beginning in a jumble of giant rocks, it rose in a series of switchbacks through fir groves and brushy clearings to emerge finally into the full sun. Wildflowers were everywhere — the cool blue of lupine, the flame of the Indian paintbrush, the purple mountain daisy, with its sunlike yellow center. As we ascended, the flowers became smaller and seemingly brighter; the more delicate white bell heather mingled with the red variety of the lower slopes. Hummingbirds darted among them. From the very tip of a solitary alpine fir a Clark's nutcracker (a crowlike bird handsomely patterned in gray, jet-black, and white) was cawing hoarsely. Peterson's *Field Guide* describes his habitat as "high mountains; conifers near tree line." He is as much a part of the open country as the gray jay or whiskey jack is of the boreal forests.

At the top of the pass we were in fact at tree line. The few remaining white spruces hugged the ground like junipers. In the shadow of the rocks lay fields of "red snow": a mysterious alga that makes the white surface seem lightly brushed with blood-red. Through the pass on the far horizon appeared a vast panorama of snow-clad peaks, the highest sliced off below their summits by a blanket of cottony cloud. On the sheer face of the nearby range the broken thread of a bright cascade led the eye upward to its source in a tiny emerald lake. The forest below showed a curious pattern of dark and light green vertical stripes; through the binoculars one could see that these were not the result of lumbering — for this is still virgin land — but of old snow and rockslides, the bright green being a carpet of new growth where the big trees had been sheared away. From a narrow ridge above the pass our lake came back into view below us: a tiny deep blue disk, shadowed and remote, like the sky-reflecting mirror at the bottom of a well.

One charm of the North Cascades is their infinite variety. Two days later we rejoined the main trail along the creek, which leads for mile after mile through a dense, dark forest of fir, spruce, cedar, and hemlock. Only the shade-tolerant flower can grow here, like the pipsissewa, with its delicate spike of pinkish blooms. Stream crossings were hazardous. Twice a laden pack mule fell flat in the mud, raising fears of broken legs. But the only result was condensation of our food supplies as raw eggs merged with the jam and the peanut butter. A deep forest is a silent place, but here — as in the Olympics, the Great Smokies of Tennessee, the Green Mountains of Vermont — a winter wren sang his canarylike song as we made our campfire. The evocative notes stretched across the miles and the years to link together those scattered moments of wilderness experience, so transient in time, so enduring in memory.

Each of our wilderness areas has its distinctive high country. In the southern Appalachians it is the mysterious openings in the climax spruce-fir forest, fringed with flame azalea, known as "balds." Alaska's Mount McKinley National Park has its rolling tundra. In the North Cascades, as elsewhere

among the Northwest ranges, the peculiar glory of the terrain at timberline is that sky-pasture known as "park." No wilderness is more welcoming to the camper, but none, alas, is more fragile, more vulnerable to overuse. When at last we left the river valley and turned onto a steep trail up the mountainside, we passed a sign: NORTH CASCADE PRIMITIVE AREA, MECHANIZED EQUIPMENT PROHIBITED. This was off bounds for scooters or "tote goats," those new destroyers of wilderness peace. The narrow path now led us up the long slope to the tableland above in an apparently endless series of switchbacks, so steep that we seemed to be riding among the treetops.

A "park" implies human origin. In this wild high country, climate and altitude have achieved the same open, almost ordered landscape: specimen trees bordering a level expanse of lush grass, beds of wildflowers so dense one hesitates to walk among them, long vistas leading the eye to snow-capped peaks. Down the center of this boggy swale a small stream meanders between banks of shining moss in a succession of miniature oxbows, suggesting a great river as seen from the air. Compared with the secret world of the forest below, life here is everywhere on display. A spotted sandpiper teeters along the stream bed, a marsh hawk quarters the meadow in search of mice, spruce grouse burst like bullets from among the evergreens. Mule deer watch us in apparent unconcern, and at night we hear the thumping of their hoofs beside our tent. At dawn we wake to the wail of coyotes.

When eventually we emerged on the western edge of the wilderness, we felt that we had only begun to know these mountains. Here are worlds within worlds. We soaked ourselves in the rain forests of the western slopes, fished clear rivers for rainbow trout, watched water ouzels in the milky glacial torrents, and made a day-long climb to a mountain lookout. And everywhere towering above us was still another world: the rock walls and alpine peaks that make the North Cascades a paradise not only for the camper but for the true mountaineer.

Paradise indeed; but we knew that if action was not taken, it would soon be paradise lost. Like the Hawaiian Islands before Captain Cook, the North Cascades survived intact through an accident of geography. The tides of change flowed around them. But with the coming of the highway, the bulldozers, the chain saws, the scooters, the "fatal impact" began. There was no sense in pretending that they could remain frozen in time: "For ever wilt thou love, and she be fair!" The question was not how to stem the tide but how to control it. Whom could the conservationists trust?

The Forest Service had a ready answer: "Trust us." Propaganda and political pressure were being used to support their claim. How valid was it? The question was relevant not just to the Cascades but to our entire wilderness system.

Unlike the Park Service, the Forest Service has from the outset been concerned with the use of our natural resources rather than simply with their preservation. In the early days of abundant land, however, its chief function was custodianship. Later, as resources dwindled, the Service became more and more engaged in management — that is, in manipulation of the environment. And its management policies have subtly changed, in fact if not on paper. The Service's much admired policy of decentralization gives maximum responsibility to the regional foresters. Ties between Service personnel and the local community are strong. Twenty-five percent of the money from timber sales is returned to the community for the support of schools and roads. On the face of it, all this sounds fine. But there is a built-in hazard. Working as he must with the leading citizens in his area, lunching with them at Rotary or the Kiwanis Club, the Forest Service official develops personal friendships and a common point of view — the view, in almost every case, of the local lumbering and mining interests. "No villain need be"; we are dealing here not with personal corruption but with the far more difficult problem of attrition through accommodation, the erosion of a theoretical ideal by the ceaseless pounding of practical politics.

"Trees must be cut down," say the lumbermen. The Forest Service has a somewhat subtler approach. Yet as Grant McConnell, a leading conservationist and authority on the North Cascades, pointed out in the *Nation,* the Service, generally recognized as one of the ablest and most independent government agencies, has gradually "had to accommodate itself to the interest groups whose activities it was supposed to regulate" — that is, the lumber industry. The cat has become custodian of the canary.

Countervailing forces are of course at work within this complex empire. The very concept of "primitive areas" and "wilderness areas" first developed within the Forest Service itself during the 1920s and 1930s. The greater part of wild America is still administered by its highly professional personnel, whose morale and technical competence are probably as high as those of any branch of the federal government. For reasons such as these, the claim of the Service to the North Cascades had the support not only of commercial interests but of many conservationists who feared the developments that a national park might bring. These groups still hoped to reach their goals through working with the Forest Service administration.

They were disappointed. In the Cascades, the Forest Service spoke too often with the voice of the lumber industry. Only such areas were recommended for preservation as were good for nothing else; wilderness, in other words, was synonymous with wasteland. When in doubt, keep it out of the wilderness system: "It may be useful someday." Those who used this argument ignored the fact that the trees in the high country are worth more as scenery than they are as lumber;

otherwise they would have been grabbed years ago. Industrially speaking, these forests are marginal. Yet the cutting went on. By the 1950s the chain saws were beginning to reach the narrow valleys and the higher slopes. Protests by conservationists were met, in the words of one patient worker in the field, with "intransigence and contempt."

As frequently happens with great organizations when they come under fire, the Forest Service countered criticism with a public-relations campaign to justify the status quo. Madison Avenue entered the woods. The campaign was built around a time-honored and superficially plausible slogan, "multiple use." On some of the most scenic roads in the North Cascades, we found signs reading: CASCADE RIVER WATERSHED MANAGED FOR MULTIPLE USE: RECREATION — WILDLIFE — FORAGE — WATER — TIMBER. In one "timber sale area" the visitor was thus informed that the cutover land would provide forage for deer, and anyway, that $37,500 from the sale was returned to the U.S. Treasury. My favorite sign, however, was the one which, after assuring the reader that the stumpland in the foreground was being replanted, drew his attention to "the snowy peaks in the background," which are "enjoyed by many wilderness travelers. This is another example of multiple use in your national forests."

There is no virtue in multiplicity unless the "uses" are mutually compatible. The *New York Times* is not promoted on the grounds that in addition to being read it can also be used for lighting fires and for wrapping fish. Logging and scenery do not go together, even when one is instructed to lift one's eyes from desecration at hand to the snowy peaks on the horizon. The mere listing of words like "water," "wildlife," "timber" is a meaningless incantation. Dams (if that is what is meant by "water") may provide some types of recreation and may also destroy a wilderness. Wildlife (as contrasted with mere numbers of deer to be hunted) achieves its maximum variety and interest in those biotic associations which have been least altered by man. Management for "multiple use" tends to be management for maximum dollar return, which is to say, for salable timber — this in a nation that no longer has a shortage of timber, but will soon be facing a shortage of wilderness.

For all its propaganda, the Forest Service in the area had not proved itself worthy of this particular trust. Was the answer, then, a national park? If so, how big and where? This time a solution was sought through official collaboration rather than through trial by combat between the Forest and Park Services. On January 28, 1963, the Secretaries of Agriculture and Interior had written a joint letter (familiarly known as the Treaty of the Potomac) to President Kennedy, initiating what they called "a new era of co-operation." Recognizing the urgent need for more recreation areas, it guaranteed that "neither Department will initiate unilaterally new proposals to change the status of lands under jurisdiction of the other Department." In short, no grabs. The joint study of the North Cascades was recommended as one of the first projects under the new treaty.

"The hard core of the issues before the study team," the report stated, "was whether there should be a new national park established in the North Cascades. Almost equally difficult questions involve the conflicts between timber utilization and recreation, and between mass recreation and dedication to wilderness . . . This report does not reflect unanimous views, because unanimity was not reached." The outcome was perhaps predictable. Two members were in favor of continued Forest Service administration, two recommended a substantial national park, and the chairman cast his vote for the compromise of a smaller park, together with establishment of new wilderness areas under continued jurisdiction of the Forest Service. Conservationists were not ecstatic over this compromise; but for the most part, with some trepidation, they put their weight behind the report.

The problem of exact boundary lines is far too complex to go into here, and anyway, maps mean little unless one has been on the spot. For example, the North Cascades Conservation Council pointed out the urgent necessity of "stopping the logging damage in the scenic heartland around the Glacier Peak Wilderness." These are just words until you see the desecration, as we did, in one of the most spectacular wild valleys in all North America. Logging or mining an area like this is like ripping the corner off a classic Chinese landscape painting. Again, when you take that unique boat trip up Lake Chelan, you realize that its shoreline is a national treasure. We believed that only a park could preserve this country, but not if the projected developments went through: roads, chair lifts, helicopters — the works. "One of the key considerations," said the report, "was that the recommendation for a park be conditioned upon its being developed for mass recreation use." Well and good, within limits; conservationists have never assumed that the national domain was their private preserve. But where would it stop? Even more disturbing than specific development proposals was the philosophy that appeared to lie behind them. Because "the volume of wilderness area use" (as the study put it) in the North Cascades has hitherto been comparatively small, we don't really need to save so much wilderness after all. This is a compound fallacy. The rate of use was going up so fast that the study team's figures were already obsolete before they were published. And in the nation as a whole, everyone knows that we are going to need more wilderness, not less. Such shortsighted reasoning ignored the whole concept of trusteeship. "Development" is a nonreversible process. Are we to leave our descendants no power of choice?

The most vocal opposition to a park was on quite different and wholly invalid grounds. Virtually every national park has been created in the face of militant local opposition. In almost every case the mood has changed to acceptance and even to enthusiasm within a few years. The basic graph is simple. Lumbermen, miners, cattlemen with grazing rights, hunters and trappers, real estate speculators all protest that a park would be the ruination of the country. Once the park is established, money begins to flow in from out-of-state tourists, new businesses spring up in the neighborhood, land values rise, and large sums of federal money find their way into the local economy through the development and administration of the park itself. The tax rate goes down, and the park is now considered the salvation of the country. Government study indicates that this process of acceptance generally requires from five to fifteen years, depending on the time lag between establishment and expenditure of funds for development. One of the bitterest fights took place in the late forties over the acceptance of a Rockefeller grant for enlargement of

Grand Teton National Park in Wyoming. Yet in Teton County, where the opposition centered, both property values and tax revenues approximately doubled in the eight years following enlargement of the park.

The study team released its report in early January 1966, just three years after it had been appointed. Public hearings — including Olympic National Park as well as the North Cascades — were held a month later. Feelings ran high. As usual, the local businessmen, the chambers of commerce, the sportsmen supported the Forest Service in opposition to the park, but there were interesting exceptions. One of the most eloquent advocates of wilderness preservation was an employee of the Boeing aircraft plant in Seattle, who had hunted and fished all his life. "Once nature's ecological system is destroyed," he said, "no amount of conservation can ever restore it . . . Should the decision be to make a national park in the area, I shall gladly give up my hunting and fishing, knowing that at least some form of protection is guarding that beautiful country from being devasted in the name of 'multiple use.' " In contrast, a local packer saw the whole thing as a scheme on the part of the Secretary of the Interior to "swallow the Forest Service." In that case, "God help us, because we would, in effect, hand over all our public lands to Mr. Udall and his arch-conservation buddies, and the result could only be utter chaos." The conservationists had a worry of a different, and perhaps more realistic, nature. A startling recommendation had been made to the Secretary by the regional director of the Bureau of Outdoor Recreation, for the excising of certain prime timber land from Olympic Park. Was this the price of local support by the lumber industry for a new park in the North Cascades? Here was a threat not only to the Olympics but to the entire national park concept. Fortunately the recommendation was not adopted and the "deal" — if such it was — never went through.

Considering the range and bitterness of the conflicts involved, the legislative machinery kept moving at a reasonable rate. On March 20, 1967, Washington's Senator Henry M. Jackson introduced a bill to establish the North Cascades National Park. Again there were hearings, as prolonged and as passionate as those on the study-team report. One such meeting that I attended was held on a warm day in late May, in the town of Mt. Vernon, fifty miles north of Seattle. The scene was Moose Hall, a barnlike structure with stage at one end. The hall was packed. Seated on the stage, flanked by his colleagues on the committee, Senator Jackson presided from 9 A.M. to 6 P.M., always on top of the subject, never losing his cool or his sense of humor, despite some extraordinary provocations. Not the least of these was the xenophobic mayor of Sedro-Woolley, Washington, whose testimony reached a climax in a long list of resentments, culminating in: "We resent that people from the outside who have never fully explored our North Cascades area should tell us what to do with it. It would take more than a lifetime for any person to see all this rugged beauty, and we could lose every member of the Sierra Club in only a part of the proposed large national park area." A loss — one felt sure — profoundly to be desired

Six months later — in November 1967 — the bill was passed by the Senate. Obviously it was compromise legislation; in the words of a leading conservationist, "it represents a substantial step forward in the drive for full protection of the area." So far so good, but the real test would come in the House of Representatives, where Wayne N. Aspinall presided over the Interior committee. The Administration bill had been introduced on April 20, 1967 (another bill, more satisfactory to conservationists, in August), but field hearings did not begin until exactly a year later. At first things seemed to go well, despite an all-out campaign in the state of Washington to kill any park legislation. (A campaign greatly stimulated by an organization with the beguiling name of Outdoors, Unlimited: a sort of holding company of "mass-recreation," anti-wilderness groups, heavily financed by local commercial interests, serving in fact as a front for the timber industry.) But as summer wore on, both park bills appeared to be stalled in the committee. "Chances of Cascade Park Action Fades," reported the United Press from Washington. "Representative Roy Taylor, chairman of a House Subcommittee on national parks, said he had received so much mail in opposition to the park that he was giving priority to other park bills." The situation was critical. Postponement of legislation until 1969 would mean starting all over again with a new Administration and a new Congress. Conservationists put on a final drive for action. At last in September the bill was reported out of committee and was passed by the House. On October 2 — together with the redwoods park, wild rivers, and national trails acts — it was signed with due ceremony by President Johnson in the East Room of the White House. A dream over sixty years old had come true.

It was real, but it was far from perfect. One major omission from the park, which I shall deal with in the next chapter, was the magnificent Glacier Peak wilderness to the south, which remained in Forest Service hands and hence, under present law, subject to mining operations. Another serious omission was the Mount Baker region to the northwest; in early 1969 a bill was introduced in Congress to add it to the park, but no action has yet been taken. In the park entrance valleys, which the Forest Service still controls, giant old growth timber is not protected from logging; to fly over these valleys, as I did not long ago, is to see how vulnerable they are to the advancing edge of the chain saws. And the very heart of the park is now threatened by the dam-building proposals of the public utility, Seattle City Light — one of which would raise an existing dam in the "recreational area" by 125 feet, inundate the access to the greatest wild area, and destroy one of the finest parts of the park.

The story of the North Cascades teaches us once more that in conservation battles there are no final victories. As I write, many vital questions are still unsettled. Public hearings were held in the late summer of 1970 on management plans submitted by both the National Park Service and the Forest Service for the areas under their control. With some reservations, conservationists were favorably impressed by both plans. The Park Service recommended that most of the park (and parts of the adjoining recreation areas) be given wilderness classification. The Forest Service plan, though making no additions to the wilderness system, and leaving some of the approach valleys still open to logging, did under public pressure recognize the recreational values of the area by recommending that some 800,000 acres be managed primarily for their roadless and scenic qualities. The timber industry, however, has mounted a full-scale campaign against any such policy, and against the whole concept on which it is based.

The issues are complex. The debate seems interminable — as indeed it is, and must be. Yet there is no better place than the North Cascades for believers in our park system to make their voices heard. Here a new park in matchless wilderness has been born. Here we can revive the practical idealism that almost a century ago made our national park concept a model for the world.

— 3 —

Kennecott Copper
and Glacier Peak

ONE OF THE most beautiful areas in the North Cascades — indeed in all northwestern America — is the Glacier Peak Wilderness. Though it was originally recommended for inclusion in the national park, the final compromise report of the study team left it under control of the Forest Service. Glacier Peak remains a controversial issue which points up, as we shall see, one of the glaring weaknesses of the Wilderness Act. Owing to the plans of the Kennecott Copper Company, it has also become the symbol of a basic conflict of values in our attitude toward public land.

As business corporations continue to grow, the distinction between private and public enterprise becomes less and less real. "Increasingly it will be recognized," wrote John Kenneth Galbraith recently, "that the mature corporation, as it develops, becomes part of the larger administrative complex associated with the State." So we are faced with the inevitable question: To what extent does a great corporation have an obligation to serve the public interest, as well as its own executives and stockholders?

Kennecott Copper, a giant second in size only to Anaconda, announced some years ago its plans for a huge open-pit mine in the heart of the Glacier Peak Wilderness. Unlike the earlier exploitation of the public domain by other companies through fraud and corruption, Kennecott's proposed action is strictly within the law. The issue is therefore more far-reaching and more complex than that of mere law enforcement. Kennecott does not, of course, own these forested ridges and snow-clad mountains; they are public property, administered by the U.S. Forest Service of the Department of Agriculture. Kennecott does, however, own 300 acres, and has unpatented mining claims on another 3000. These claims were staked out under our free-and-easy mining laws at the turn of the century, and taken over by a Kennecott subsidiary some ten years ago. Under the Wilderness Act of 1964, areas officially designated as wilderness are protected from lumbering, road-building, mechanized travel, or from any other use incompatible with their pristine character. But prospecting is still allowed until 1984 (as it is not in a national park) and previously existing mining claims can be exploited. Like a buried bomb that hasn't been defused, this situation has haunted conservationists, who have wondered when and where the bomb might go off. Now they know.

The Glacier Peak Wilderness is vulnerable on another score. Until recently few persons outside the Northwest were aware that these American Alps existed. Far fewer have enjoyed the superlative view of Glacier Peak itself from the proposed mine site at nearby Miners Ridge — a view described as "the scenic climax of the entire North Cascades." Offering no immediate economic opportunities, the area has been ignored. Yet once modern technology has made its exploitation commercially profitable, it will be saved only through concerted action by an informed public.

Fortunately there are precedents, on the part of both individuals and corporations, for putting public interest ahead of private profit when unique natural values are concerned. One of the earliest and most famous is the public-spirited action on the part of the explorers who discovered the wonders of the Yellowstone, almost a century ago. Had they staked out personal claims and managed these rare geological phenomena as a tourist attraction, they would doubtless have made a handsome profit. Instead, following the precedent set in Yosemite Valley a few years earlier, they urged the then novel idea that the area be administered by the federal government for the enjoyment of all the people. Yellowstone thus became our first national park.

Unhappily, we cannot automatically expect such self-denial, least of all on the part of great corporations. As their directors are quick to point out, the stockholders' money is involved. To be sure, when there are many stockholders they constitute a sizable segment of the interested public, as do the company's potential customers. Accordingly, even if it were legal and otherwise desirable for the Ford Motor Company, let us say, to build an assembly plant in the middle of New York's Central Park, the company would surely desist, both from a sense of public responsibility, and because the sale of Fords in the Manhattan area would be likely to fall off. Unfortunately, this principle applies only to a product with a trade name. Customers for copper tubing, for example, cannot be expected to know what company mined the ore, or

what future public assets it may have destroyed in the process.

Nevertheless, great corporations are jealous of their public image and spend many millions to keep it fresh. Paper companies have recognized the recreational value of their vast timberlands, and on occasion have refrained from cutting along rivers and highways; even the ruthless exploiters of our virgin redwoods were forced to save some trees for a national park. Several years ago the world's largest public utility, Pacific Gas and Electric, abandoned its plan for an atomic power plant at Bodega Head north of San Francisco after a bitter fight by conservationists; later, the same company had second thoughts about locating a plant on southern California's beautiful Nipomo Dunes. In the face of determined local opposition, B. F. Goodrich Chemical Company withdrew its request to locate an industrial plant on the banks of Maryland's famous Chesapeake and Delaware Canal. And Little Stony Point in the Hudson River highlands was saved when Georgia Pacific Corporation voluntarily chose another location for its gypsum wallboard plant, after acknowledging that the scenic values of the original site could not readily be ignored. On the same river, Consolidated Edison may ultimately be prevented, through a new interpretation of public interest by the courts, from building a power plant at Storm King.

Federal agencies have made similar concessions. In the most publicized of all conservation battles, the Administration withdrew support for bills authorizing construction of dams in the Grand Canyon. And as we shall see in the next chapter, on the far-off coast of northwestern Alaska, where it might be (and was) assumed that one could get away with anything, the all-powerful Atomic Energy Commission abandoned plans for its bomb excavation experiment, Project Chariot, when the effect on the region became publicly known.

Kennecott's excavation plans for Miners Ridge involve nothing quite so dramatic as atom bombs, but there are resemblances. Since the ore is low grade, only an open-pit mine is economic. "Hopefully," as their vice president in charge of mining, C. D. Michaelson, put it, there will be "thirty years of blasting." This would create a crater almost half a mile in diameter and five hundred feet deep, high on the ridge, reached by fifteen miles of access roads, through an area classified as wilderness. A mill would be constructed and tailings dumped into the valley below; waters would be polluted and probably poisoned. All this at the very core of the National Park–Wilderness Area complex!

The news of this impending disaster broke late in 1966. Protest was immediate. The Sierra Club and the North Cascades Conservation Council, long aware of the threat, went into action. The Governor of Washington, speaking officially for his state, and the Secretary of Agriculture came out against the project. This is a case, said Secretary Freeman, "of balancing a priceless, yet intangible, national treasure against ledger sheets and profits . . . The scenic values of this area are as well known to the company as they are to you and me. The company can, if it so chooses, ignore these values; gouge out its road and begin operations . . . But I cannot really believe that such an application will ever reach my desk." Some of Kennecott's own stockholders protested at their annual meeting. The company has had a standard reply to all criticism: "Of course we're going ahead and mine. You can't desert property." They admit that Miners Ridge would be a tiny percentage of their total operation, but they fear the precedent. "If we are stopped here and in half a dozen other places that we plan to develop," says Mr. Michaelson, "then we would have to go out of business." Pressed further, they fall back on the sure-fire plea that it is essential to the war effort: "Have you a son in Vietnam?" Alas for Kennecott, this argument has already backfired. Miners Ridge would produce less than one-half of one percent of the annual U.S. consumption of copper. Freeman said flatly, "Our present war effort will not suffer if Miners Ridge is left undeveloped. Neither will our civilian standard of living suffer."

The final, unanswerable opinion came — amazingly — from the Department of Defense. Assistant Secretary Paul R. Ignatius wrote to Senator Henry M. Jackson, Chairman of the Committee on Interior and Insular Affairs: "Because of the length of time necessary to bring the mine into production and the relatively small amount of additional copper that would result therefrom" it is doubtful that its contribution would be "sufficient to outweigh other important considerations, such as the inevitable damage to the natural beauty of the wilderness area."

So the lines are drawn. The outcome at Miners Ridge in the North Cascades may well become as decisive in the nation's conservation battle as was Gettysburg's Cemetery Ridge in the Civil War. A bloodless victory is still possible. The chief of the Forest Service has already recommended legislation empowering the government to buy up mining claims at a fair price. Kennecott may, in fact, want to unload its mining claims on the government; its threat to the wilderness — which has succeeded in arousing national concern — may be simply a move toward a profitable settlement. On the other hand, Kennecott may be fronting for the whole industry in seeking a test case of the mining provisions in the Wilderness Act — realizing that, if they are allowed to go ahead, no wilderness area will be secure.

In most aspects of modern life our great corporations have been forced to accept the obligations that go with wealth and power. Education, arts and letters, public health, elimination of air and water pollution have all come within their pattern of responsibility. Should preservation of natural beauty alone be excluded?

The Kennecott issue, though momentarily dormant, is not dead. "Any day we may wake up to a new crisis at Miners Ridge." Such was the reluctant conclusion of a young student and conservationist, Benjamin A. Shaine, who in April 1969 went to the top executives of the company with a petition from ecologists and environmental experts pointing out the irreparable damages that would result from their proposed operation. The response was unequivocal: whenever it could be shown that the mine was profitable (and copper prices were rising) they would go ahead. The principal reason given was that the balance of payments would be helped by any little bit of additional domestic copper. And anyway, hadn't the decision already been made by the Wilderness Act, which allows mining? "President Milliken evaluated the power of conservationists as 'small peanuts.' Public pressure through legal channels, publicity, or extra-legal means is not a major factor in Kennecott's decision, he said. Mining division chief Michaelson added: 'At least they don't eat you in the Northwest.' Apparently Kennecott has faced rather violent opposition from tribesmen at some of their other sites."

Though hampered by our social customs from taking such direct action as Mr. Michaelson suggests, conservationists do have weapons to oppose the destruction of the Glacier Peak Wilderness. And one of the strongest, despite Mr. Milliken, is growing awareness of the public responsibility of the private corporation.

— 4 —

The Disturbing Story
of Project Chariot

IN ALASKA everything from the price of eggs to the antlers of moose is more than life size. Even Texans have to admit that it is, geographically, our largest state, though they may shrug off this fact with the inaccurate comment that most of it is covered with ice. It contains, of course, the greatest remaining areas of wilderness in North America. And as one might expect, the threats to this wilderness are of a comparable magnitude. One would have to travel as far as the Florida Everglades to find so fragile an environment under such deadly attack.

The oil strike in the far North has created the most immediate and extensive threat of all, but it is by no means the first. In considering the current crisis in Alaska, something can perhaps be learned from the story of the two major exploitation projects of the late fifties and sixties, which also involved both the rights of the native peoples and the rights of the land itself. There were the Atomic Energy Commission's Project Chariot and — to be described in the next chapter — the plan to drown the Yukon Flats.

The Chariot story is peculiarly disturbing as an illustration of the secrecy and cynicism (and initially also ignorance) with which a powerful government agency may work. Little was known about it in the early planning stages, though it was certainly dramatic enough: an attempt to blast out an artificial harbor with atomic bombs. The lack of publicity for this bold and questionable idea — a pioneer experiment in the peaceful uses of atomic energy — was partly a matter of geography. In 1958, when the project got under way, the eyes of the American public were not focused on Alaska as they are today — and certainly not on a little-known strip of coastline in the far Northwest. If the Atomic Energy Commission had proposed to set aside an area half again the size of Rhode Island somewhere in the continental United States, if it had proposed to detonate nuclear explosions which would affect the immediate livelihood and traditional property rights of several hundred farmers or cattlemen, if there were one chance in a thousand that the radioactive fallout would contaminate cattle ranges or commercial fisheries, the story would have made banner headlines.

But Point Hope, the Eskimo village that would have been most affected by the blast, is farther from Washington, D.C., than is the coast of Africa; and its unaggressive inhabitants, as they quietly went about their business of living, doubtless seemed remote from our daily concerns, though they were citizens of the United States.

Point Hope is a village of about three hundred Eskimos, at the tip of a long spit of land projecting into the Chukchi Sea north of Bering Strait, some hundred miles above the Arctic Circle. (In Eskimo the land spit is called Tigaraq, which means "index finger.") In continuous existence for at least 5000 years, the village is one of the most successful communities in the Arctic. To quote a student and friend of the Eskimos, who spent a winter at Point Hope: "It is successful because a talented and vigorous people have harmonized the cultural patterns of the modern European-American and the traditional Eskimo." Unlike most northern villages, Point Hope depends very little on state and federal welfare support. Summer employment and sale of native products supply the cash for guns and gasoline and other outside necessities, but it is essentially a hunting economy, wholly dependent on the fish, seals, and whales of the nearby waters and the game animals — principally caribou — of the immediate hinterland. It is also a delicately balanced economy, closely synchronized with the rhythm of nature. Like the farmer, the man who hunts for a livelihood must gather his crop under certain conditions, at certain times of the year. But his domain must be far wider; he must be free to travel over limitless stretches of undisturbed range, in pursuit of game that is always on the move.

My wife and I visited this vast roadless area in July 1961, when the project was already in full swing. We flew in with a bush pilot who has operated for many years from Kotzebue, the "Eskimo capital of Alaska." (At the Kotzebue airstrip stood a station wagon marked "Project Chariot.") As we looked down on this magnificent country from a few hundred feet, we could see, widely scattered amid the subtle greens and browns and ochers of the gently rolling tundra, an occasional sharp white accent marking the site of an old caribou camp. At the moment most of the caribou were

farther north, but we saw grizzly bear and moose. Then we dropped down for a bumpy landing along the bank of the Noatak River, where our pilot left us to camp for a few days, to enjoy the silence and to get the feel of the summer Arctic.

This is the Eskimo homeland. For the Point Hope Eskimos, a principal hunting ground is the Ogotoruk Creek Valley, near Cape Thompson, about thirty miles southeast of the village. During one season 95 percent of their caribou meat and almost all of the village's freshwater fish were taken within twenty-five miles inland from the mouth of the creek. This was the spot which the Atomic Energy Commission had chosen for a chain explosion of five atomic bombs — one of them ten times the size of that dropped on Hiroshima.

Was this a desirable plan? The question seemed open to

debate. Since 1959, the Point Hope Village Council had objected to Project Chariot, and on March 3, 1961, the Village Health Council wrote President Kennedy that it opposed Project Chariot because the blast would be "too close to our homes at Point Hope and to our hunting and fishing areas":

> All the four seasons, each month, we get what we need for living. In December, January, February, and even March we get the polar bear, seals, tomcod, oogrook, walrus, fox, and caribou. In March we also get crabs. In April, May, and June, we hunt whales, ducks, seals, white beluga, and oogrook. In July we collect crowbell eggs from Cape Thompson . . .
>
> The ice we get for our drinking water during the winter is about twelve miles off from our village towards Cape Thompson.
>
> We read about "the cumulative and retained isotope burden in man that must be considered." We also know about strontium 90, how it might harm people if too much of it get in our body. We have seen the Summary Reports of 1960, National Academy of Sciences on "The Biological Effects of Atomic Radiation."
>
> We are deeply concerned about the health of our people now and for the future that is coming.

Quite apart from any immediate risks to the Eskimos and their means of livelihood, the principles involved were so fundamental as to seem to require, in the absence of a national emergency, that the American people know what was going on, and that the decision not be left entirely in the hands of a governmental agency. What information could one get on which to base an intelligent judgment? The official statements were confusing. Was the plan to create a harbor, as originally announced, or wasn't it? Was it an economically self-supporting venture for the people of Alaska, as originally announced, or simply an experiment in nuclear excavation? Could the experiment (in the words of the Atomic Energy Commission) "be conducted without jeopardy to the local inhabitants or to the plants and animals from which they derive their living," while at the same time a principal object of the test was to determine "the effect of nuclear excavation on the biota (i.e., living things)"? Did the federal government have the legal right to withdraw 1600 square miles (not 40 square miles, as originally announced) from the Eskimos' traditional hunting grounds, guaranteed at the time of the Alaska Purchase? To seek answers to these questions we must turn back to the beginning of the project.

On June 19, 1957, the Atomic Energy Commission had established the Plowshare Program for exploiting peaceful uses of atomic energy. But the program lacked a definite experimental goal. Russia's launching of Sputnik I on October 4 put the heat on the American scientific community to produce an impressive technical breakthrough. By November, Lawrence Radiation Laboratory scientists at the University of California recommended to the AEC that earth excavation offered the "highest probability of early beneficial success" in the Plowshare Program, and by year's end they had designed a massive explosion equal to 2,400,000 tons of TNT, to be known as Project Chariot.

After some consideration of other ideas, the physicists set-

Alaska:
Sites of Project Chariot
and Rampart Dam

Sam¹ H Bryant

tled on a plan to blast an artificial harbor — or at least a hole that could be made to look like a harbor — at Cape Thompson, on the northwestern coast of Alaska. The AEC asked the U.S. Geological Survey for a study of the geologic and oceanographic factors relevant to blasting a harbor on the Alaskan coast between Nome and Point Barrow, later amending its request to include a detailed report on the twenty-mile coastal strip south from Cape Thompson. Meanwhile the Laboratory contracted with the E. J. Longyear Company for a study of the "economical mineral potential" of the coast. No travel to Alaska was authorized for either study.

In April both reports came back. The Geological Survey found that "the northwest coast of Alaska is relatively unknown geologically" while the Cape Thompson area is "largely unexplored" and is ice-locked nine months of the year. But the Longyear report concluded that in twenty-five years a port at Cape Thompson would handle "substantial" amounts of oil and coal, which it indicated were in abundance near the Cape. Both reports were based on published sources rather than investigations at the spot.

Chariot was gaining momentum. On June 5, 1958, Lewis Strauss, then chairman of the AEC, requested the withdrawal from the public domain of 1600 square miles of land and water in the Cape Thompson area. Four days later the AEC publicly announced Chariot, saying that "the absence of harbors on the northwest coast of Alaska close to important large-scale mineral deposits has in the past hampered development of such deposits." It added, "Fishing in this area has also been impeded by the lack of a safe haven." The shot was set for 1960.

Dr. Edward Teller, director of the Lawrence Laboratory, led a group of scientists and AEC officials to Alaska a month later to raise support for Chariot. "We looked at the whole world — almost the whole world," before choosing Alaska as the site, he told a meeting in Juneau. "The blast will not be performed until it can be economically justified. It must stand on its own economic feet over a long-range period." Speaking in Fairbanks, he said nuclear explosives could be so controlled as to "dig a harbor in the shape of a polar bear, if desired." He said it was up to the Alaskans to choose the site of the blast and assured his audience that two thirds of the $5 million spent on the project would be spent in Alaska. On the day Dr. Teller spoke in Fairbanks, his associate director was already at Cape Thompson with a group of bomb experts, surveying the bed of Ogotoruk Creek, where it was soon decided that Project Chariot would take place.

The Alaskan press threw itself into enthusiastic support of Chariot as a lucrative federal project which would put the new state on the world map. Congress had passed the Alaskan Statehood Act just a few weeks before. The *Fairbanks News-Miner* wrote, "We think the holding of a huge nuclear blast in Alaska would be a fitting overture to the new era which is opening for our state."

But business leaders were skeptical of the alleged mineral deposits and the need for a harbor. A few members of the science faculty at the University of Alaska, a handful of citizens, and several key government officials questioned Dr. Teller's assertions that the blast would be safe. The northwestern coast is not uninhabited; the Geological Survey report showed that in the 1600-mile coastline from Nome to

Barrow there are only eleven spots as much as twenty miles distant from any human habitation. The Alaskan dissenters demanded that the AEC establish a scientific basis for its assurances that Chariot would not harm human life or livelihood.

Soon the AEC itself lost faith in Chariot and announced that the project was about to be dropped for lack of support in the state. The new chairman, John A. McCone, testified to the Joint Committee on Atomic Energy: "We are seeking an alternate to the harbor in Alaska because, as I said to this committee once before, we couldn't find a customer for the harbor." Alaska's Senator Edward L. Bartlett, checking into the confused picture, said that "no one on the Commission staff concerned with this believed for a minute private capital would, in the foreseeable future, invest money in this area merely because an artificial harbor had been created . . . I have now been completely disillusioned. If there is such absolute lack of co-ordination within the Commission in planning, goodness knows what would happen when the trigger were pulled. For one, I hope the AEC does its blasting elsewhere."

It was a critical moment. After building up such a head of steam, was Project Chariot going to be sidetracked after all? Obviously it had not been properly "sold" to Alaska's citizens. The physicists at the Lawrence Laboratory recognized the crisis. Two of them toured the new state, warning that Chariot's fate depended on endorsement by chambers of commerce and by the state legislature. Newspapers took up the campaign, urging citizens to write their chambers of commerce to "vote yes" on Chariot. A second group of scientists concentrated on the legislature in Juneau and on business groups in major cities. By mid-March 1959, Chariot had the backing of the Fairbanks Chamber of Commerce, with others falling into line, and an official endorsement from the legislature. The AEC quickly reaffirmed its confidence in the project. The engine was back on the track.

Preparations were resumed at Ogotoruk Creek, and it was assumed that the blast would sooner or later go off. What, specifically, were the ends to be accomplished and the risks involved? Press reports still referred to Chariot as "the harbor project" — though geologists estimated that a few coastal storms would seal off the mouth of the excavation with sand and gravel. No mineral deposits had been found "suitable for commercial exploitation." But, announced the AEC, "it was decided to continue investigation of the site with a view to conducting the project as an excavation experiment, even though the harbor probably would not be commercially useful." Like Proteus, the Old Man of the Sea (who would have taken a dim view of this tampering with the borders of his domain), Chariot changed into something else the minute you thought you had a grip on it.

The stated purpose was now to obtain "additional data on . . . crater-producing nuclear detonations." Useful information, no doubt, but far from the project's original goals. Was this another case of decision by inertia — the very human inclination to go ahead with any plan that has the momentum of much money and many man-hours already committed to it?

The question of risks was still harder to resolve. By wading through a morass of scientific technicalities, one could find, if not a definite answer, at least some of the reasons why such an answer was impossible. This should have surprised nobody. Project Chariot was quite frankly an experiment; and the essence of experiment is uncertainty. Let's phrase the question differently. What sort of risk were we talking about? And did that delicate balance of life at Cape Thompson, which in turn was so closely tied in with the life of the Eskimos, allow any margin for uncertainty?

Our limited experience with atomic blasts elsewhere was not definitive here. The frozen ground of Alaska might be affected quite differently from the soil of Nevada or New Mexico; for example, a dust cloud of finely pulverized material might greatly extend the area of fallout. One recalled Project Gnome, the supposedly "contained" underground explosion that went awry, bursting out of its deep shaft and releasing a stream of radiation across the desert. In short, no one knew, not even the experts.

They did know that the "food chain" on the arctic tundra is peculiarly susceptible to radioactive fallout. The flesh of the Alaskan caribou contains about seven times as much strontium 90 as the meat of domestic cattle in the rest of the United States. Why? Because caribou feed on lichens — rootless plants that derive their nutriment from the dust in the air as it is carried down by rain and snow, thus directly absorbing radioactive fallout before it becomes diluted in the soil. The Eskimos feed on the caribou. Obviously they are already subject to greater intake of strontium 90 than the rest of us. Another danger from the Chariot explosion was of concern to conservationists everywhere as well as to the local Eskimos. The sea cliffs north of Cape Thompson constitute

one of the principal nesting areas of several specialized species of seabirds: common murres, thick-billed murres, black guillemots, pigeon guillemots, horned puffins, tufted puffins, glaucous gulls, and kittiwakes. Altogether they number over 200,000 individuals, and their eggs form a regular part of the Eskimos' diet. These sea cliffs are the product of slow wave erosion; they are unstable features, peculiarly vulnerable to earthquake shock. If they should be partly destroyed by the effect of the blast, the available breeding habitat of these highly specialized birds would be greatly reduced.

Biological studies, prompted by the Alaskans themselves and generously financed by the AEC, have shown how rich and varied are the flora and fauna of this apparently empty land. Over 300 species of plants (including rare species of

Asian origin) and 21 species of mammals have been found in the Cape Thompson area, ranging from the collared lemming to the grizzly bear and barren ground caribou. The first pre-shot surveys ever undertaken by the AEC, these studies constituted a milestone in policy. Unhappily, there was bitter disagreement over the assessment of the reports; one botanist quit the project on the grounds that "the Environmental Committee was merely going along with the predetermined policy of the AEC." According to the official press release, there was no biological reason for stopping or deferring the project.

The Eskimos did not agree. A large area of their best hunting grounds would be affected. Camping would be impossible so long as the hunters' source of water for drinking and cooking — melted ice or snow — might still be contaminated. This interruption could mean virtual loss of a whole season's hunting and meat supply, and consequent dependence on welfare support and alien foods, with a lasting effect on their culture. As a matter of fact, for the first two years of Chariot's career, the residents of Point Hope, Noatak, and Kivalina were silent and almost forgotten. Not till the spring of 1960 did official representatives from the AEC visit the Eskimo villages to explain Chariot. The members of the Village Council of Point Hope remained unconvinced by the assurances offered to them. At the conclusion of the meeting they voted unanimously to oppose Project Chariot.

In November 1961, representatives from Eskimo villages up and down the coast met at Point Barrow for a conference on native rights, sponsored by the Association on American Indian Affairs. Project Chariot was discussed. The confer-

ence claimed that the Chariot site belonged to the Eskimo
people, that the Bureau of Land Management had no right
to license the AEC to do research there. It called on the
Interior Department to revoke the license. The Alaskan
Eskimos were at last beginning to make themselves heard.
Listen to the opening of their report:

> We the Inupiat have come together for the first time
> ever in all the years of our history. We had to come
> together in meeting from our far villages from Lower
> Kuskokwim to Point Barrow. We had to come from so
> far together for this reason. We always thought our
> Inupiat Paitot [aboriginal hunting rights] was safe to
> be passed down to our future generations as our fathers
> passed down to us. Our Inupiat Paitot is our land around
> the whole Arctic world where the Inupiat live.

The words, the very cadence, have a familiar ring. Hearing them, one's mind turns back a century and more to the
days when the American Indian was fighting for his aborig-
inal rights. Few of us can recall that story without a sense
of guilt, even though we tell ourselves that it was a choice
between us and them, between grass for longhorn cattle and
grass for the buffalo. The Alaskan Eskimos offer no threat to
our way of life. How far must we inevitably be a threat to
theirs?

For the conservationist, the story of Project Chariot has
a happy ending. The opposition of the Eskimos, who refused
to be taken in by the salesmen for the AEC, the rising tide of
public indignation as the truth about the scheme came to
light — these eventually forced the government to put the

project on the shelf. Chariot "may well be dead," wrote the *New York Times* on May 13, 1962: killed by adverse publicity of the effect on the Eskimos, and the wildlife on which they depend.

But if Project Chariot is dead, the idea behind it is not. Thwarted in its attempt to set off its explosions on the mainland, the AEC has transferred its experiments to Amchitka Island in the Aleutians, the great breeding ground of the fur seal. And elsewhere in Alaska, the native peoples are still fighting for their rights. Less than a decade after the demise of Chariot, their ancient homeland is being threatened on all sides by the impatient forces of "progress." Once again powerful interests are pressing to carry through, without adequate scientific study, projects that may change the face of the earth in ways that are still unknown.

— 5 —

The Plot to Drown Alaska

As any small boy knows, the presence of running water is a compelling reason to build a dam. Most boys when they grow up turn to other things, but a select few go on to join the U.S. Army Corps of Engineers. Here, under the heading of flood control, navigation, or power production, they build dams beyond the wildest dreams of youth. Some of these dams are necessary and some are not; all of them provide jobs for the Engineers. Most of them involve huge expenditures of federal money. The biggest, most expensive of all is the plan to dam the mighty Yukon River at the Ramparts in east-central Alaska, creating the largest artificial lake in the world.

To the layman, the name Army Engineers, as the Corps is usually known, suggests activities concerned with the military. This is logical but inaccurate. The Army Engineers, consisting of the elite of West Point (originally established as an engineering school), have a superb military record, but most of their work has nothing to do with war. They are the most independent executive division of our government.

Engaged largely with "improvement" of navigable rivers and harbors, they have access to the biggest chunks of pork in the barrel, and they are beloved by Congress. They have, on occasion, successfully defied the President. Yet in all their glorious history they have never had a chance quite like this to show what they can do.

Here, in brief, is the plan. A glance at the map on page 65 will show its magnitude. The Yukon River, which rises in the Yukon Territory of northwestern Canada, crosses 1300 miles of Alaska from east to west, flowing northwest from the Canadian border to touch the Arctic Circle at the town of Fort Yukon, thence west and south to empty at last into the Bering Sea.

Best known as the gold-miners' route to the Klondike, its place in Alaskan history suggests that of the Ohio, Mississippi, and Missouri river systems in the opening of the West. Now, alas, the great stern-wheelers, reminiscent of Mark Twain's days on the Mississippi, lie rotting on the riverbank at White-horse, wood-hungry engine stilled, proud pilothouse a nest for swallows. But in a changing world, where leisure gives more time for recreation, where a burgeoning population needs room to breathe, the Yukon has taken on a new importance. To conservationists, the most valuable part of the entire river is the area known as the Yukon Flats, which extend approximately from the town of Circle, now reached by an extension of the Alaska Highway, downstream 300 miles to Rampart Canyon, northwest of Fairbanks. Over 100 miles wide, this vast network of sloughs and marshes and potholes provides, in addition to its fur-bearing population, one of the finest wildfowl breeding grounds in North America.

To the Corps of Engineers, this presents a golden opportunity. By building a single great dam at the narrows, they could put the entire Yukon Flats under several hundred feet of water. They would thus create a lake with a surface area greater than Lake Erie or the state of New Jersey. The lake would take approximately twenty years to fill. The dam, 530 feet high and 4700 feet long, would cost, at lowest estimates, $1⅓ billion. The money would come from the federal government. Though over a million dollars has been spent in preliminary engineering surveys, the principal flow of money would start when and if the dam is voted by Congress.

The sales campaign behind Rampart, which began in the early sixties, was a promoter's dream. Starting out with a $100,000 budget, an organization called Yukon Power for America was formed for the sole purpose of pushing Rampart through Congress. YPA included businessmen, newspaper publishers, chambers of commerce, the mayors of the principal cities in the state. There was even a junior membership for schoolchildren at twenty-five cents a head.

YPA's first publication was a colorful brochure entitled *The Rampart Story*. The claims were not modest. The basic one was, of course, cheap electrical power. By providing electricity at three mills per kilowatt hour, the dam would, according to YPA, attract industry — notably the aluminum industry — to Alaska.

Furthermore, "once lured to Alaska by Rampart's mass of low cost energy, several industries would find new uses for the state's coal and gas reserves." The reservoir itself would "open vast areas to mineral and timber development," and provide unlimited recreational potential. Sixty million dollars

a year would be spent on construction alone, and "new workers with their families would more than double the population." In planning this paradise YPA had widespread support beyond that of the Engineers who first launched the project. The Golden Valley Electrical Association was solidly behind it. An organization called North of the Range termed Rampart "Alaska's future . . . We have to come forward with both guns blazing."

A sense of now-or-never hung over the battlefield. "We are going to have to do a tremendous selling job," said the mayor of Fairbanks. The mayor of Anchorage agreed: "The political climate is favorable now for the project. I feel that if it is not built now, it probably will not be built." Congress, as one YPA official put it, feels "an obligation to the new state."

Senator Ernest Gruening was equally frank in addressing the state legislature at Juneau. "Alaska is confronted with the task of catching up after years of federal neglect. We were excluded from the federal aid highway program, and virtually excluded from federal aid power projects." It was also a matter of catching up with Russia, where he had seen "hydroelectric power dams larger than the largest in America."

The senator's administrative assistant, George Sundborg, author of a book on Grand Coulee Dam entitled *Hail Columbia,* not only reflected this urgency but gloried in the speed with which things were moving. "The sun shines bright on it." Grand Coulee, he recalled, required years of study. "And here we are practically ready to start the dirt flying on Rampart."

Simultaneously he castigated the Interior Department's Fish and Wildlife Service for speaking against Rampart "without waiting for the evidence to come in." "To be realistic," Sundborg said, "what can we expect of a Department whose Secretary seems to conceive of his mission as dealing primarily, if not exclusively, with parks and recreation" — and who was off climbing Mount Kilimanjaro when he should have been pushing for Rampart in the McKinley Park Hotel? Representative Ralph Rivers went further. The time had come to have "a heart to heart talk" with Udall. "I should think that Stewart has a few punches coming, and I can see that we have adequate talent on the [Alaska] delegation to administer those punches."

When an army takes the field under such dynamic leadership, questions of fact are roadblocks to be swept aside. It is good for morale to simplify the issue: "Are you for ducks or for people?" and to sneer at the opposition: "Do we," said Mr. Sundborg, " — please excuse the metaphor — have all our ducks in a row . . . ? Far from it. Rampart has its enemies — waiting with a loaded shotgun and a red-hot mimeograph machine."

Employing a novel criterion for assessment of land values, Mr. Sundborg dismissed the entire area to be drowned by the dam as worthless; it contains "not more than ten flush toilets." After exploring the region for over a week by small boat and by plane, I challenge this estimate; the figures are grossly exaggerated. The Yukon Flats are wholly without plumbing. This is wild country, and its values are wilderness values. To get a fair impression of it, one must visit not only the Flats themselves but the river from the Canadian border

down to Tanana, since the Army Engineers' long-range plan includes two dams in addition to Rampart, one of which would back up the water as far as Dawson in the Klondike.

A small group of us made this trip in the summer of 1964, launching our two flat-bottomed, scowlike "Yukon River boats" — twenty feet long, with outboard motors — at Eagle and finishing ten days and 650 miles later at Tanana, situated on the river below the Rampart Dam site. Eagle was the first incorporated town on the Yukon. The Army base, with a garrison of 2000 at the turn of the century, had the responsibility of keeping law and order along the river. Still standing are the huge stables for the Army mules. Nearby, lining the riverbank, is an Indian village; the native people are Athabaskan Indian, not Eskimo. The river here is already broad, swift, and brown with silt, bordered by alluvial flats or steep cliffs of limestone and shale. Camping the first night opposite a dramatically beautiful bluff, we could hear the current swishing past its base with the rush of a brook in spate.

Next morning, as the early mist began to burn away, we let the motors sleep and drifted. The only sound was the hiss of silt against the boat, like the finest rain on an attic roof. Near the mouth of a tributary, whose clear blue waters met the muddy Yukon in a sharp line, a cow moose stood placidly with a yearling bull at her side. Flocks of mallards congregated near the shore, and somewhere from a slough echoed the cries of red-throated loons. Though in August we were too late for the nesting season, we saw more and more waterfowl as we approached the Flats: pairs of widgeon, small flocks of white-fronted geese, and two sandhill cranes, long necks outstretched and wings beating slowly as they flew directly overhead.

Later on, when we had reluctantly started the motor, we drew alongside another cow moose swimming the river, and marveled at her power and speed as she fought her way across the current, the water parting at her straining neck and shoulders and bubbling whitely over her barely exposed withers. This is prime moose country. We counted ten the first day on the river, including several old bulls with that great spread of antlers which makes the Alaska moose one of the most impressive creatures in the world. America's largest land animal, it is the chief source of meat for the native peoples in many parts of the state. This is wolf country, too.

These much maligned animals, so necessary to the balance of nature in the Arctic, have not yet been exterminated along the Yukon, as they have over so much of their former range. In the mud at the water's edge their round tracks, like those of huge dogs, mingled with the print of the moose's sharp hoofs — though only once did we get a glimpse of this living symbol of the wilderness.

Above the Flats, signs of human habitation were few. An occasional trapper's cabin, a channel marker from the steamboat days, an Indian family's summer encampment, where salmon were being caught in fish wheels, dried on racks in the sun, and smoked in rough frame shelters like tobacco sheds as winter food for men and dogs. If every river has its voice, the voice of the Yukon is the rhythmic groan and *plosh* of these giant wheels turning slowly in the current, their webbed baskets now and then scooping a silvery fish from the thousands pouring upstream. Nowhere in the world do salmon ascend rivers for such distances as they do in the Yukon system. Now in August, over a thousand miles from the sea, the king salmon had already gone by, but the silver-salmon run was at its height, and dog-salmon were yet to come. Visiting with an Indian family, we sampled the "squaw candy" made from choice, delicately smoked strips of king salmon, which fetch a high price at Fairbanks and points south.

At the town of Circle the character of the river changes. Here the Flats begin. The main stream becomes diffused in a maze of secondary channels, sloughs, eddies, shallows, and dead ends, which once or twice baffled even our native Indian boatman. It moves as swiftly as elsewhere, but is broken by ripples and torn by snags and sawyers (one always thinks of Mark Twain) rhythmically rising and falling in the current. The hills have been left behind; the tablelike bog stretches to the horizon (not very distant when your eye is just above the water), relieved occasionally by an isolated bluff, such as the one where we met an archaeologist and his staff from the University of Alaska who were unearthing traces of an ancient Indian settlement. They shared the site with a pair of peregrine falcons, aristocrats of hawks from the days of chivalry. As we climbed up to watch and photograph one of the two young — still tufted with white down but learning to fly — the falcon circled and shrieked overhead, while her mate, the tiercel, perched restlessly nearby. The peregrine falcon has ceased to breed in the eastern states, owing to the sterilizing effect of pesticides. The few birds we see in the East are raised, like these, in the Arctic. For how long?

From the peregrines' eyrie we could look far out over the Flats, as the early men who lived there must have done to spot their game. But to read this vast landscape, one must, like the peregrine, fly over it. Our opportunity came at Fort Yukon, whose airstrip, since the decline of river traffic, is its connection with the outside world. All day we flew in a single-engine plane, adding a third dimension to our surface view of the past few days. The first impression was that of a giant abstract painting with muted colors and swirling shapes. Actually it is a picture in imperceptibly slow motion. Wherever there is a current, teardrop sandbars are growing into islands, tinted here and there with green as the willows take hold. Bends cut off by the ever-shifting river are left

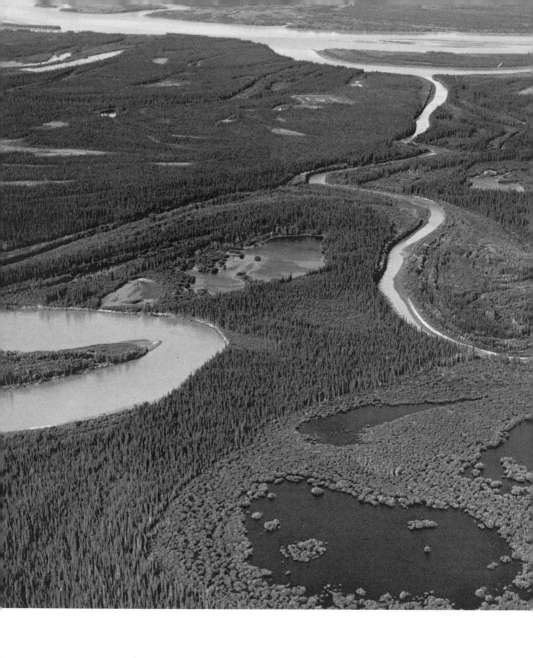

as oxbows of still water. The key to the more distant past —
to earlier and long abandoned riverbeds — is the pattern of
vegetation. Since spruce grows best on the higher, better-

drained ground of the natural levees built along its edge by the river itself, one can trace the course of successive channels by the concentric curves of spruce forest. There are

ponds of every size and shape, deep blue in contrast to the
coffee-colored river, bordered with bright green sedge. So
clear was their water that, flying low, we could make out
moose tracks crisscrossing the mud of the bottom.

There are estimated 36,000 lakes and ponds on the Yukon
Flats, the area which, if Rampart Dam is built, will become
one huge windswept lake. This abundance of shallow water,
of grasses and cattails and aquatic vegetation, makes ideal
breeding ground for waterfowl. Such country is vanishing
fast, both in the United States and Canada. Despite agricultural surpluses, we continue to drain our marshes to make
more farmland. Wheat farms and settlements are relentlessly
encroaching on the famous pothole country of Canada's
Prairie Provinces, where the great bulk of our waterfowl now
breed. In the light of these facts, are the Yukon Flats, which
contribute as many ducks as the entire "lower forty-eight"
states, worth saving? Shift the camera back to Fairbanks,
Anchorage, and Washington, D.C.

"Search the whole world," continued Mr. Sundborg (following his vain search for flush toilets), "and it would be difficult
to find an equivalent area with so little to be lost through
flooding." Rampart's supporters were impatient with what
they called "the old, old arguments of professional conservationists" — as if truth somehow decayed with age. Others
brushed off "this duck business" with wisecracks such as "Did
you ever see a duck drown?" "Anyway, if the ducks don't like
it, they are smart enough to go elsewhere." Just where is not
specified; other breeding areas are already being used to
capacity. Some birds that breed on the Flats migrate to

Siberia; are we, asked an officer of YPA, going "to mollify these feathered defectors?" Officially, YPA took the matter more seriously, but offered reassurance: "Despite some early fears of wildlife and fish displacement in the reservoir area, available evidence shows no significant effects." This statement is so outrageously untrue that one must in charity call it a supreme example of the public-relation man's power of wishful thinking.

The official report on the Rampart project by the U.S. Fish and Wildlife Service to the Corps of Engineers stated flatly: "Nowhere in the history of water development in North America have the fish and wildlife losses anticipated to result from a single project been so overwhelming." A nesting habitat which contributes annually about 1,500,000 ducks, 12,500 geese, and 10,000 little brown cranes to the four North American flyways would be completely destroyed. The resultant lake would provide no substitute. "The fluctuating reservoir would have steep, wave-washed shorelines which would preclude formation of marshes suitable for nesting or shallow waters productive of waterfowl foods. The large expanse of open water would provide no nesting habitat."

What of the salmon run? At least 270,000 salmon pass the damsite annually on the way to spawn in the upper waters of the main river and its tributaries. If Rampart is built, fisheries upstream will be totally destroyed and, with the loss of the upstream spawning grounds, the product of the entire system drastically reduced. Fish ladders for such dams have been proved impractical, and fantastic schemes for trapping the salmon and transporting them upstream in barges not only would be prohibitively expensive but would not work anyway, since the fry would never find their way downstream through several hundred miles of dead water.

What about other wildlife? The moose range, with an estimated eventual carrying capacity of 12,000 animals, would of course disappear. So would martens, wolverines, weasels, lynx, muskrat, mink, beaver, otter, which taken together represent an annual harvest of some 40,000 pelts, or about 7 percent of the entire Alaska fur production — a sizable item to write off in any state's economy, which is, nevertheless, far below the future potential. The report concludes: "We strongly oppose authorization of the Rampart Canyon Dam and Reservoir project."

Last, but certainly not least, what of the people who live along the river? Seven villages in the Flats would be drowned; some 1200 natives would be evacuated; the livelihood of 5000 to 6000 more in Alaska, and an estimated 3500 in the Yukon Territory, would be affected by the reduction of the salmon run. After a quick flying trip to the area, Senator Gruening reported that most of the natives he talked to were in favor of the project. My impression was somewhat different. I did find two articulate supporters of Rampart. One, an elderly native resident of Fort Yukon, thought that the building of the dam would provide jobs for his numerous sons; the other, a white trader at Rampart Village, felt sure that he could get a whopping price from the government for his establishment and retire in luxury. But this did not, I think, represent the majority view. I detected a reluctance on the part of these people to having their homeland obliterated, to being located elsewhere with no means of livelihood, to spending the rest of their lives on relief. To be sure, there

was a feeling of fatalism; if the government wants the dam, they will build it — what can we do?

I wonder whether the senator may have confused this resignation with consent. At a meeting of village leaders in Fort Yukon they expressed themselves against the Rampart project. The village council of Venetie, an independent self-respecting community north of Fort Yukon (which, unlike the latter, has very few people on relief) voted unanimously against the project. Perhaps they did not agree with the senator that they live in "an area as worthless from the standpoint of human habitation as any that can be found on earth." It may be expedient to displace these native people and drown their towns for the greater good of the state as a whole. But let's not pretend that they like it.

Below the dam the effects could also be disastrous. At present, the seasonal flooding of the river replenishes the marshy shores and pothole lakes, which in turn support the furbearers, the moose, the waterfowl, and the fish on which the Indians depend. Their whole way of life may be destroyed if the dam is built. Rampart's backers speak confidently of the jobs that would be created by this vast construction project. But no technical training program has been established for the native people. Who would get the jobs, untrained Indians or construction workers brought in from the "lower forty-eight?"

The sun may once have been "shining bright on Rampart," but many areas have always been in shadow. All one can say for sure is that the losses, tangible and intangible, would be immense. Can the gains justify the cost? What in fact has been the true source of support for this glorious project of the Army Engineers?

The ostensible purpose is hydroelectric power: power in huge quantity at low rates. Not, in this case, to meet a demand that already exists. Alaska needs power, but it neither needs nor can use it on any such scale as Rampart would provide. The approach has been from the opposite direction. Unlike Grand Coulee Dam on the Columbia River, where contracts for the use of the electricity preceded construction, Rampart is a speculative venture. If the dam were built, could the power be sold?

A number of economic studies have been commissioned to provide the answer. Three of them are particularly illuminating. In 1961, the Battelle Memorial Institute made a twenty-year projection of Alaska's development. It found that "tourism offers the most promise for immediate and continuing returns to Alaska." Major mineral developments are conjectural. As for power production, "future energy-use in Alaska will be characterized by increasingly keen competition among hydro, coal, gas, and oil, and possibly nuclear in the farther future."

In January 1962, Arthur D. Little, Incorporated, of Cambridge, Massachusetts, delivered its report to the State of Alaska. It had examined the industrial possibilities of petroleum, natural gas, coal, and electric power. To Rampart's boosters the report came as a shock. "Regarding the larger hydroelectric projects, it should be noted that it is not correct to speak without qualification of low-cost hydroelectric power. Low-cost for any particular project must be accompanied by high-volume use. The larger hydroelectric projects proposed for Alaska as capable of providing 2 or 3 mill power would . . . produce a quantity of power many times the ability of present Alaskan industry, commerce and population to absorb."

Rampart is a 5-million-kilowatt project. "At its present stage of development even a tie-in with all smaller industrial, commercial and domestic power markets would not fully utilize a hydroelectric project with an excess of 1 million kilowatt capacity unless several electric-intensive industries appeared on the scene within a short period of time. This is, of course, a possibility but not a very realistic expectation."

This was not the sort of talk that the politicians and the Army Engineers wanted to hear. What to do? As quietly as possible the report was filed away, though news of it did leak out. Meanwhile, the Army Engineers had proved equal to the crisis. Realizing in advance that the A.D.L. study was not going the way they wanted, the Engineers, in consultation with Rampart's promoters, commissioned another report, from the Development and Resources Corporation of New York, to deal specifically with the market for Rampart power. No time was wasted: the new report was issued within a year — only three months after the other — and printed by the U.S. Government Printing Office. Its conclusions were much more satisfactory. "Based upon the marketability of Rampart power and the benefits resulting from its use, as indicated by our analysis, our study affirmatively suggests: A decision to move ahead soon with the Rampart project will prove nationally prudent, wise and desirable." This was more like it. The D. and R. report was given the widest possible distribution and instantly became the Bible of the Let's Build Rampart Now movement — though critics have suggested that it reads more like the prospectus for a bond issue.

Both studies were, of course, preliminaries. In February 1965, the "field report" of the Department of the Interior, which has jurisdiction over the project, was released. Though it avoided final judgments, the facts set forth were cold comfort to the promoters and the Army Engineers. The thesis that low-cost power will necessarily lead to resources development was not valid. The timber industry would not benefit; on the contrary, over one billion board feet — three years of Alaska's current timber production — would be destroyed.

Several alternative sources of waterpower would cause far less damage than Rampart: Wood Canyon on the Copper River, the Yukon-Taiya project near Skagway, and, most immediately practical of all, Devil's Canyon on the upper Susitna River between Fairbanks and Anchorage. The latter project was officially approved by the Department of the Interior in 1961. It would provide more than adequate power for Alaska's immediate needs, while causing virtually no damage to its wildlife or other natural resources. As an alternative to Rampart, Devil's Canyon has the strong support of Alaska's conservationists.

Most significant in the long view is the prospect of cheap nuclear power, which would make Rampart obsolete before it was built. In any case, with labor rates among the highest

in the world, with the heavy costs of transportation over such great distances, central Alaska does not in fact offer an irresistible lure to the aluminum or any other industry. What if the dam were built and the lure should fail to work? In that event, say Rampart's rooters with a certain note of desperation, we'll ship the power south to where it's wanted, ignoring the fact that this would require the passage of high-power lines across Canadian territory. Since British Columbia takes the view that it has enormous power potential in its own province, much closer to American markets, the chances of any such arrangement are dim indeed. Canada's Minister of Northern Affairs and National Resources, Arthur Laing, has made clear his country's opposition to such power lines. "We do not think that undertaking is desirable on all the known facts," he says of the Rampart plan.

Alaska would in any case lose most of the long-term benefits.

Rampart would provide hydropower in abundance. What else? Water storage and irrigation are the last things this area needs. "Primitive values" would of course be wholly destroyed. This leaves only recreation among what they call the multiple uses. *The Rampart Story* makes a big thing of the recreational potential of the 280-mile-long lake that would be created: "Fresh water boating and sailing . . . hunting lodges and fish camps on scenic shorelines . . . marinas, dock and float plane facilities — all accessible by rail, highway and air."

Let's see. The lake would be on the Arctic Circle, at the same latitude as Great Bear Lake. At a guess the ice would break up in early July. High winds and waves on a body of water this size require seagoing vessels. The lake would be filled with dislodged timber, the shores strewn with debris. Since the country is almost flat, the drawdown at the damsite could create a mile of mudflat between the "marina" and your boat. Hardly the perfect recreation area.

So, finally, we come to the immediate motive behind Rampart Dam. The achievement of statehood brought problems to Alaska. Taxes went up, and there were relatively few sources to tap. For twenty years, the building and manning of military installations, including the famous DEW Line, had channeled vast amounts of federal money into the area. Then the defense boom tapered off. Gold mining and the salmon fishery were on the downgrade. Thus, at the very moment of transition between territory and state, Alaska was facing a downsliding economy. Employment needed a shot in the arm. The dam would have poured a minimum of $1\frac{1}{3}$ billion into Alaska, and probably a great deal more. As one legislator is said to have remarked privately, Rampart Dam will have served its purpose if it is blown up the day it is finished.

From the start, Rampart Dam has been a colossal make-work project: a huge federal subsidy for a once shaky state economy. The discovery of oil on the north slope, in 1968, in spite of all its resultant ecological problems, has at any rate taken Alaska out of the poorhouse. The real motive behind Rampart no longer exists. But the project had for other reasons already ground to a halt before the oil strike in the north; the guns were no longer blazing, and the dirt never did begin to fly. A study team of the Council of Natural Resources presented a report strongly opposing the dam on both ecological and economic grounds. The Interior

Department finally said no. In the light of this opposition, backed by an increasingly well informed public, the chances of getting an appropriation bill through Congress dwindled to nothing.

Has the battle for the Yukon been won? (Is any conservation battle ever won, once and for all?) The Governor of Alaska and former Senator Gruening still hope that Rampart Dam will be built, though they admit that the outcry of the conservationists, which did so much to spoil their plans, will make the project hard to revive in the near future. Beneath all the shouting, all the hucksterism lie honest differences of opinion. But the question that concerns us is bigger than the dam itself, with its ten million cubic feet of concrete; it is bigger even than the state of Alaska. The very magnitude of such a project brings home to us the terrible responsibility that goes with the possession of limitless technical means for controlling nature. How far does a financial speculation like Rampart Dam justify us in permanently changing the face of the earth?

— 6 —

Super Jetport
or Everglades Park?

H UMAN HISTORY," wrote H. G. Wells, "more and more becomes a race between education and catastrophe." A precise illustration of his thesis, in terms of land use, is the huge jetport that was to be built in the heart of the Florida Everglades. Promoted by the Dade County (Miami) Port Authority, backed by four major airlines, by the Federal Aviation Administration, by local boosters and land speculators, it threatened the very existence of that unique subtropical wildlife paradise, Everglades National Park. Thirty-nine square miles in extent, it would have been big enough to contain the Los Angeles, San Francisco, Washington's Dulles, and New York's Kennedy airports with room to spare. The land was condemned and work begun on training runways at the intended location only six miles north of the park boundary. "A new city is going to rise up in the middle of Florida," said Alan C. Stewart, director of the Dade County Port Authority. "You are going to have one whether you like it or not." If he had been right, the impact on the surrounding country would have been devastating. Local speculators would have gotten rich; but Everglades National Park, which belongs to all the people, would have been doomed.

To understand the seriousness of the threat, one must be aware of the special conditions in southern Florida. Socially, politically, and geographically it is a region of extremes. Population is exploding; by the year 2000, Florida will probably be the third largest state in the union. Real estate development is booming; traffic by road and air is increasing at a fantastic rate. Pressures on the land and water are at a maximum; zoning for their protection at a minimum. The politicians and promoters (often indistinguishable) are everywhere calling the tune. The physical environment, on the other hand, is extraordinarily fragile and vulnerable to misuse. In short, the greatest alteration of the landscape anywhere in the southern United States was being imposed on the area perhaps least prepared to withstand it.

Where did the proposed jetport fit into this picture? Unfortunately, in dead center. Looking at the Florida peninsula as a finger extending into the sea, the vast expanse of Lake Okeechobee lies roughly at the final joint; the Everglades run south down the center of the peninsula from there to Cape Sable and Florida Bay. West and north lies the Big Cypress Swamp. To the east, like a long curving fingernail, extends the rim of rock that forms the Atlantic coastline, protecting the fresh water of the Everglades from the salt water of the ocean. Here are concentrated the seaside resorts and burgeoning cities. Here, dominating all, is Miami.

As anyone who has visited or read about Everglades National Park knows, the Everglades consist of a vast, shallow,

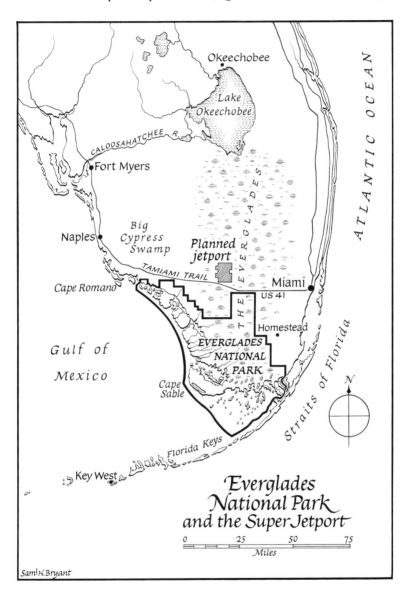

Okeechobee

Lake Okeechobee

CALOOSAHATCHEE R.

●Fort Myers

ATLANTIC OCEAN

Big Cypress Swamp

Naples●

Planned jetport

TAMIAMI TRAIL

Cape Romano

US 41

●Miami

Homestead

Gulf of Mexico

EVERGLADES NATIONAL PARK

Cape Sable

Straits of Florida

N.

Florida Keys

Key West

Everglades National Park and the Super Jetport

0   25   50   75
Miles

Sam! H. Bryant

slow-moving river: Pa-hay-okee, or Grassy Water, as the Indians called it — reminding New Englanders of the Indian name of Musketaquid, or Grass-Ground River, for Henry Thoreau's beloved Concord. Fresh water moves south and southwestward from the region of Lake Okeechobee, reaching the boundary of the park some seventy miles to the south where U.S. 41, the Tamiami Trail, runs due west from Miami. When left to its own devices, the water flows under the highway and on through the park to empty eventually into the Gulf of Mexico. On this seasonal flow (southern Florida, though technically north of the tropics, has the tropical pattern of wet and dry seasons), the entire character and life of the park depends.

The fight for the use of this water, that is to say for the existence of the park, has recently received national publicity. Directly north of the Tamiami Trail lies Water Conservation Area 3-A, managed by the Central and Southern Florida Flood Control District and the U.S. Army Corps of Engineers. As the president of the National Parks Association pointed out, these conservation areas, like the park, "serve as a habitat for a teeming plant and animal life, subtropical in character, of immeasurable scientific, esthetic, ecologic, scenic, and human value, which can be found nowhere else in the United States."

During the severe drought of the early 1960s, the floodgates along the highway were closed; the local farmers got water for irrigation, while the park dried up. When Lake Okeechobee was full again, water desperately needed for the park was diverted directly to the sea. Endless negotiations with the Army Engineers and state authorities still have not resulted in a firm agreement to allow Everglades National Park its share of water.

Obviously a huge airport — not to mention "a new city in the middle of Florida" — would make the water problem infinitely more acute. The site chosen, close to the border of the park, lies in the southeastern corner of the Big Cypress Swamp, bordering the Conservation Area. Two of its runways would be six miles long, to accommodate the supersonic transports and other flying monsters of the future. A corridor to Miami, 50 miles long and perhaps a quarter of a mile wide, would bring fuel by pipeline, supplies by road and rail, and bodies in transit (estimated at 50 million per year) by some as yet undetermined speed device (lest they spend more time between city and airport than they spend jetting halfway around the world). Landings and takeoffs would eventually average one every 30 seconds around the clock.

To service this frenetic activity, and to make sure that the expected golden rain fell on southern Florida, developments of every sort would inevitably have arisen from the surrounding saw grass and cypress. Indeed they were greedily anticipated and prices went skyrocketing when the site became known. Speculators began organizing drainage districts to "improve" the land between the jetport and the park. "I'll make you a bet," said Alan Stewart in the fall of 1968, "that five years from now the hotels will be there." He was delighted at the prospect. "Let's do something big enough for a change."

What would this mean, in terms of the region as a whole? "Slow death," said Park Superintendent John C. Raftery succinctly. "Portions of the park literally face ruination." It is shocking but true that there had been no coordinated attempt to determine scientifically the impact of the airport, much less the surrounding development, on the total environment. Yet one needs only a rudimentary knowledge of ecology to realize the consequences of such a concentration of men and machines on a vast man-made island in the heart of a swamp. Can an area of perhaps 150 square miles be drained for urban and industrial subdivision without affecting the quantity and quality of water flowing through the Everglades? Pollution is inevitable. How much and how deadly cannot be estimated, but enough is known to make one shudder. For example, on takeoff a jet plane discharges about a gallon of unburned fuel into the air. When the airport was in full operation, two gallons a minute would rain down on the water and vegetation of the Conservation Area that lies just beyond the runway. Add to this all the chemical wastes associated with any large maintenance and servicing operation. Worst of all, visualize the effluent, domestic as well as industrial, produced by a city whose eventual population might reach over a million — along with the pesticides used to keep down the mosquitoes, the herbicides sprayed along the roadways, the fertilizers running off in Florida's torrential rains.

Nor could the results be confined to the neighborhood of the city. The entire environment "downstream" — which is to say all of central-southern Florida — would be subject to creeping death. This is not just horrid fantasy; serious effects have already been observed. Replacement of one type of algae by another is already taking place, and pesticide levels found in the tissue of fish taken from the park are already alarmingly high. Concerned with "the far-reaching effect on the entire environment of south Florida" of the jetport and satellite developments, state and federal conservation agencies and private conservation groups addressed over a hundred questions about environmental control to the Dade County Port Authority. The answers added up to a litany of evasion: "This is under study," "Cannot be answered at this time," "Study in progress at this time," "No study of this type has presently been started," "No such studies have been conducted . . ."

The slow poisoning of the air and the water may escape attention, but evolution has not yet produced a human being insensitive to the roar of jet engines, much less to a sonic boom. The Port Authority, aware of complaints from residents near the existing Miami International Airport, has had the effrontery to designate Everglades National Park a "sound screen." "The park and Conservation Area 3 are sound barriers in that no human habitation in these areas is anticipated." Spokesmen for the aviation industry have been even franker: "Favorable noise environment of the 39-square-mile site is indicated by large undeveloped areas, with Indian reservations, Everglades National Park, and state water conservation areas serving as buffers . . ." The training field already being built, and known to some airline officials as the "Green Corn Dance Airport" from the Indian ceremonies associated with the area, was expected to permit twenty-four-hour training operations because of the "absence of neighbors to complain about the noise." Though the flight plan called for planes to gain altitude (when they are at their noisiest) directly over the park, the Federal Aviation Administration's Miami area manager was not concerned. "Nobody will be close enough to complain

except, possibly, alligators." Except, possibly, the Indians who have lived there for generations, and the one million annual visitors to the park, whose chance for a wilderness experience would be gone forever.

My wife and I had the opportunity to visit the unique wilderness of the Everglades when the jetport controversy was at its height. We explored this largely roadless area from two opposite poles: from a low-flying plane and from a canoe along the canals and tortuous waterways of the great mangrove swamp.

With its pusher-propeller mounted above the fuselage (powered, I am convinced, by rubber bands), the tiny, quiet plane gave an unobstructed view of the flat expanse of saw grass stretching to the horizon. I could think of nothing to compare it with but the arctic tundra. Out of the brown grass rose countless islands of green: hammocks and bay-heads, each an individual forest community. With their axes parallel to the flow of water (the largest hardwoods generally at the north or upstream end) these islands of vegetation reminded me of the willow-clad teardrop islands on the Yukon Flats. The crisscross tracks of airboats through the grass might have been the trails of migrating caribou. But the first sign of bird-life brought us back to the subtropics. The water was deep for early April; about belly-high to a great blue heron. Flocks of white and glossy ibis and wood storks were constantly on the move; a group of black-necked stilts stood in the mud near the Tamiami Trail. Then, just north of the park boundary, came the shock: a slash across the wilderness as if a strip of skin had been torn from a living body. This was to be the site of the airport for "the superjets of tomorrow." Bulldozers and trucks were at work; great rectangular holes in the saw grass showed where the fill had been dug out. Here the term "rape of the land" was no longer a figure of speech; it was a visible fact. And this was to be just the beginning . . .

Not till we had turned south and finally lost sight of this man-made desecration did the sense of wilderness peace return. Below us was a cypress forest; then as we approached Florida Bay the dense jungle of mangrove. Small streams joined to form a larger "river," which to a northern eye looked more like an irregular chain of connected lakes, suggestive of the Quetico-Superior canoe country. Here a layer of slow-moving fresh water flows over the salt water from the bay. Where the two meet is the great food-producing area of the Everglades, nursery for shrimp and countless other forms of life — a unique habitat wholly dependent on the supply of pure fresh water from the north. As we reached the bay, we spotted a mature bald eagle perched on a snag. A few hundred yards off shore lay a school of porpoises, clearly visible as they rested beneath the waves. Heading home, we dropped low to watch the aerial maneuvers of an Everglades kite and circled a large alligator resting by a water hole, undisturbed by our passage. The kite's-eye view had been rewarding. Next we would try the alligator's.

To paddle slowly along the canals and "canoe trails" of Everglades Park is to get a sense of the country that is impossible to achieve from the highway. As one penetrates deeper and deeper into the mangrove forest, the whine of speeding cars fades away; the only break in the silence is the occasional squawk of a heron, momentarily disturbed from his fishing at

the water's edge, or perhaps the rattle of a kingfisher or the shrill cry of a red-shouldered hawk circling overhead. Wherever there was an opening in the mangroves, we would get an intimate view of the birdlife that makes the Everglades a birders' paradise: a variety of herons, egrets, and ibis on the mudflats; the dark back of a limpkin barely visible among the stiltlike roots of the mangrove; flocks of blue-winged teal, scooping up food from the shallow water almost like spoonbills; a brown pelican watching us, unconcerned, from the top of a tall dead tree. Black skimmers sliced the surface of the canal with their knifelike bills. Most spectacular of all were the roseate spoonbills, now in their rich spring plumage. They went on feeding, indifferent to our presence, straining out minute particles of food from the opaque brown water with quick sweeps of their fantastic bills as they crossed and recrossed the lagoon.

In addition to the canals, the Park Service has marked out canoe trails that lead into the heart of the lake-dotted wilderness that we had seen from the air. Imagine entering a watery maze, where the trail, or sometimes tunnel, worms its way through the mangrove thickets, at times no wider than the canoe itself. At every turn — which is to say at about every third stroke of the paddle — our respect grew for the water-woodsmen who had laid out this tortuous trail, using bits of red cloth in lieu of blazes. After an hour or so we had learned only one principle of navigation: the obvious route is *never* the right one.

Little by little the openings grew larger. One last turn and we emerged onto a broad, windswept lake, where a bit of dry ground beneath a young palm had been cleared for a picnic site. So far we had traversed only the outer chambers of the labyrinth, for the trail led on and on. But in less than a two hours' paddle from the highway we already felt that we were deep in the wilderness so vast and strange as to seem a world of its own.

Is this wilderness doomed? Unlike other Port Authority officials, the director has been brutally frank. If the wilderness and wildlife are to be protected, "the conservationists had better start saving up their pennies around the country and buy the land." As he well knows, the conservationists don't have that many pennies. Neither does the National Park Service, which ideally should have acquired the land at the time the park was established. The Port Authority's pennies, however, are safely invested. Another comment by Mr. Stewart was even more revealing: "If the airport doesn't develop the way we think it will, we'll have twenty square miles of real estate we can sell off. It will still be a good deal."

What then was to be done? Had ecological disaster again won the race against education? Not quite. The boosters and speculators were far in the lead, but they still faced the hurdle of public opinion. If the people hadn't raised their voices, it was because they hadn't known what was at stake — or had been baffled into silence by a churned-up political scene as obscure to the outsider as a squirming alligator hole in the dry season.

The proposed jetport site lies at the juncture of Collier, Monroe, and Dade Counties. Collier County has one city, Naples; most of the rest is cypress swamp, already spawning the worst type of "development," from poachers' shacks to colossal real estate ventures. Here Gulf American Corporation is "building new worlds for a better tomorrow" on a 100-square-mile tract christened "Golden Gate Estates." "The wilderness has been pushed aside," the promoters boast, "with calipers and slide rules . . . draglines and dynamite rigs . . . we are literally changing the face of Florida." Monroe County, less fortunately blessed, consists only of the Florida Keys and a bit of land north of the park. This has left Dade County, which is to say Miami, at the controls. The Dade County Port Authority had been flying high, but flying by the seat of its pants — without ecological studies, without even a master plan for the area. Through arrangement with the other counties, Dade was to control the jetport area. For the rest it would take no responsibility, and neither would anyone else.

The land for the jetport was condemned, and construction began on the training airport with a $500,000 grant from the Department of Transportation. As a biologist at the University of Miami pointed out, "the environment has already been drastically changed." "The engineers who are engaged in construction are not concerned with environment planning," stated the Port Authority. The Authority said it was "in negotiation with an entirely independent Overview Group to provide advice on preservation of the existing environment." Flight operations were scheduled to start long before these studies were completed. Yet by admission of the Authority itself, sites for the training port had been under consideration since 1957.

"Facts," wrote Winston Churchill, "are better than dreams."

Not in Dade County they aren't. Soothing words are safer. Richard H. Judy, deputy director of the Port Authority (and formerly comptroller of the State Road Department), assured conservationists that their interests would be protected. He didn't say how. By discussing the problem piecemeal with the various agencies involved — the Flood Control District, the Game and Fresh Water Fish Commission, the Federal Aviation Administration (no trouble there!), the State Board of Conservation, etc. — he built up a fine file of letters of

consent, each being concerned only with the "jurisdictional
areas for which this agency is responsible." (Mr. Judy did slip
up once when he apparently sponsored a highway to Miami
straight through the holdings of the Flood Control District.
This was too much. "I am extremely sorry," he wrote to its
chairman, "that one of the suggested 1–75 corridors that runs
through the middle of Conservation Area 3 was even located
on the map which I used as an exhibit in my presentation to
you.") "Jurisdiction" is the key word here. Without some
overall control, Mr. Judy's lullaby leads only to nightmares.
"Dade County Port Authority has no responsibility or jurisdiction for off-airport areas . . . this will depend on controls
by other appropriate agencies." What agencies? "If the
affected agencies are involved in coordination with the Port
Authority," wrote a representative of the federal Bureau of
Outdoor Recreation, "they are quite unaware of it."

The Port Authority's objective was, and still is, the economic
development of southern Florida. In the deputy director's
own words (alas for consistency) it is not confined to the airport area. In a letter to Arnold Ramos, district engineer of
the Florida State Road Department on November 8, 1968,
Judy urged "that we move with great speed" in planning the
transportation corridor. He went on to say that "four of
the world's major airlines are standing by to help implement
the final engineering concepts . . . If we can establish this
schedule we can promote new air industries to locate in Dade
and Collier counties." Where but in "off-airport" areas, for
which "we" have no responsibility? Meanwhile the Miami
office of the Federal Aviation Administration, while doing
lip service to "compatibility with park interests," could not

contain its enthusiasm. "The start of this airport is a great event for southern Florida. When you think of what New York, Chicago, New Orleans, or Los Angeles would give for such an opportunity . . ."

The local interests knew what they wanted and they were determined to get it; the fate of a national park was not their concern. But where had the federal government been all this time — specifically, the Department of the Interior and its agency, the National Park Service? The Park Service has stated that the Port Authority's search for a jet training site first came to its attention "early in 1967" (ten years after the search, according to Mr. Judy, had begun), and that "subsequently, the plans were enlarged to include regular commercial operations, including SST's." Deeply involved in the apparently endless struggle to assure water for the Everglades, park officials were slow in recognizing the new menace of the jetport, and accepted at face value the assurances that park values would be protected. "Don't be concerned," was the line taken by the Port Authority, "we'll consult you before we pick a site."

The site was actually chosen for all practical purposes in the late fall of 1967, when Dade County got the right to acquire land in Collier County; there had been no approval from the National Park Service. On December 20, 1968, the superintendent of Everglades National Park wrote as follows to the director of the Port Authority (showing that the Park Service, like the rest of us, only knows what it reads in the papers): "A recent news column by Mr. Clark Ashe of the *Miami News* states that the Port Authority has demonstrated it has been clearing its moves with the Flood Control District,

Everglades National Park, and other conservation-minded agencies for many months. I was aware of and pleased by the series of meetings initiated by your design firm to develop the problem areas resulting from the jetport development. The initial development at the jetport site is now proceeding rapidly, yet, to my knowledge, we have not been advised how the Authority proposes to resolve any of those matters of concern that evolved from the meetings. Since the jetport has the potential for a significant and perhaps disastrous effect on Everglades National Park, I am concerned that we have not been included in further planning or advised regarding your proposed solution to the very serious questions that have been raised."

The layman who is accustomed to think of the United States government as a fairly powerful protector of the nation's heritage gets quite a jolt when he reads the account of a meeting that took place on February 27, 1969 (high time!), in Miami between representatives of the Interior Department, the Central and Southern Florida Flood Control District, the Sierra Club, and the National Audubon Society to determine, among other things, what position the Department should take at the public hearings the following day. It was decided that "strong arguments should be avoided" and that the presentation of "the facts concerning the federal government's interest and involvement would only show the weakness that the government has in achieving proper planning and control measures for the preservation of the Everglades area." Whatever the "weakness" of Interior's position (we shall come to this shortly), the shocking fact remains that no formal statement concerning the jetport had been made up to this time to the Dade County Port Authority by the U.S. government.

Were the people of the United States to remain powerless in the face of a determined local pressure group? Not, in this case, if the Secretaries of Transportation and Interior were willing to intervene. Section 4(f) of the Department of Transportation Act requires the Secretary of Transportation to cooperate and consult with the Secretary of the Interior in developing any transportation project. Furthermore, "the Secretary [of Transportation] shall not approve any project or program that requires the use of publicly owned land from a public park, recreation area, or wildlife and waterfowl refuge" unless there is no feasible and prudent alternative and unless such a program includes all possible planning to minimize harm to such a park. By the Port Authority's own admission, Everglades National Park was to be used as a climb-out area and as a sound buffer. The harm to the park was obvious. The state conservation and recreation area would also be used as a sound buffer, and for surface transportation to Miami. No one can claim with a straight face that there had been "all possible planning to minimize harm," either from intolerable noise or from pollution, or that all feasible and prudent alternatives had been explored.

On April 23, 1969, a meeting which represented "practically the entire conservation and environmental movement in the United States" addressed a letter to the Secretary of Transportation pointing out the damage that a jetport on the projected site would cause to the national park and state conservation area, and stating the belief that the Secretary "is in a position to settle this question" without need for any

legislative action. Then in early June, Senator Henry M. Jackson of Washington, chairman of the Senate Committee on Interior and Insular Affairs, held hearings on what he termed a "classic case history" of the impact of modern technology on the environment. The purpose was "to review the process of federal decision-making which has contributed to the conflicting patterns of federal, state, and local land use which presently threaten the Everglades National Park" — and, by extension, to demonstrate the need for the legislation he had introduced to establish a national environmental policy.

Under questioning from the committee, there emerged an amazing pattern of confusion and frustration in high places: confusion because each branch of the government had been acting (or failing to act) independently; frustration because the federal government, having neither an environmental policy nor the police power for enforcement, finds itself at the mercy of state governments whose machinery is even more archaic, and who are therefore in turn thwarted by local authorities whose single goal is economic development, and who can proceed on their own as long as they can raise the money. It soon became clear that no high-level discussions had ever taken place between the Interior Department, the Department of Transportation, and the State of Florida before the jetport site was chosen; that the Port Authority and the Federal Aviation Administration had not even seriously attempted to bring state or federal conservation agencies into the making of the decision. Other sites with a less damaging impact on the ecology could have been found. As an ultimate absurdity, one such site had been rejected because the counties involved could not agree on the allocation of landing fees.

The Everglades jetport is an abortive offspring of the unholy wedlock of the booster and the engineer. It represents the same philosophy that allows industry to pollute air and water to the brink of disaster, agriculture to use poisons like DDT long after the hazards are known, the Army Engineers to dam rivers and dig canals with no concern for the total environment. The peak of such folly was almost achieved, not surprisingly, in the Everglades country, when the Corps of Engineers decided to "pull the plug" in Canal 111 to see whether the result would be as disastrous as ecologists claimed. Fortunately the latter were alert. A frantic weekend of calculations with a computer showed that the whole area would be covered with two feet of salt water. The plug is still in place. But the philosophy endures: you are an alarmist until you can be proved dead. The Corps of Engineers, for example, does not want to "make an issue" of park water needs "until the situation gets tight." The Corps claims that it has no legal right to establish regulations to provide the park with water. The Department of the Interior disagrees; it believes that regulations should be set up now. During the Senate hearing, the then Undersecretary, Russell E. Train, criticized the plan of the Corps as one "to invite growth, and then struggle with the results later."

The present priorities of the Corps and of the state are clear: people first, agriculture second, Everglades National Park third — if there is any water left over. "You can grow as long as you can steal water from the park," remarked Senator Gaylord Nelson of Wisconsin, pointing out that we are producing with federal money far more water than the park is asking for. "We don't have to sit here and be clobbered by the State of Florida." Turning specifically to the problem of the jetport, he concluded that we had only two alternatives: either stop it at the chosen site, "or we publicly admit that we are going to destroy the park." As a matter of fact, many state and local political leaders shared his concern.

Could it be stopped? The Department of Transportation admitted at the Senate hearing that transportation programs are on a collision course with environmental management. Interior promised to "do everything in its power" to stop the jetport if it was satisfied that either the training field or the commercial airport would destroy the park. On April 30, 1969, a special assistant to the Secretary of the Interior had

written: "As regards other Park System problems, I can only say that no single problem approaches in seriousness the threat posed to Everglades National Park by the proposed Miami jetport. We are in the process of arranging studies to determine what adverse effects will occur and what measures are realistically available to reduce these effects to tolerable levels. The studies may reveal, however, that the park and the jetport will not be compatible, in which case relocation of the proposed jetport will be the only solution."

Following the Senate Committee hearing, a federal-state "task force" was finally appointed to make technical studies that should have been started much earlier, before any site was selected. Publication of its report some months later marked a turning point in the struggle. The findings of the research team supported the conservationists' position unequivocally: "Development of the proposed jetport and its attendant facilities will lead to land drainage and development for agriculture, industry, housing, transportation, and services in Big Cypress Swamp that will destroy inexorably the south Florida ecosystem and thus the Everglades National Park." Even before the report appeared, the Secretaries of Interior and Transportation and the Governor of Florida had agreed that the main jetport would have to be located elsewhere. As of this writing, no alternative site has been selected. And the training field is now in operation, despite the conclusion of the task force that it is "intolerable" because, without proper land-use controls, it is bound to result in further land speculation and development.

The battle to save the Everglades is not over. Nor is it only of local significance. As the official report states so wisely, "The south Florida problem is merely one example of an issue that sooner or later must be faced by the nation as a whole. How are the diffused but general costs to society to be balanced against the local, more direct, and usually monetary benefits to a small portion of the society?"

— 7 —

Oklawaha: "The Sweetest Water-Lane in the World"

"Five miles meandering with a mazy motion
Through wood and dale the sacred river ran . . ."

S AMUEL TAYLOR COLERIDGE, so far as I know, never
    paddled a canoe, but in "Kubla Khan" he caught the
dreamlike quality of Florida's spring-fed rivers as only a poet
could. Alph, the sacred river, was of course conceived in a
dream (so rudely interrupted by "a man from Porlock") but
it was firmly based on a factual description by one of America's earliest and greatest naturalists, William Bartram, in his
classic *Travels.* That the journal of a botanist in the Florida
wilderness should have inspired one of the great poems of
the English Romantic Movement is of more than purely lit-
erary significance. It is a dramatic symbol of the change in
the attitude toward wild nature that took place quite suddenly in the closing years of the eighteenth century. Wilderness, hitherto considered alien and hostile, entered our culture
as a source of inspiration and a road to truth. In "conquer-
ing" a continent, Americans have lost that road more often

than they have followed it. But we are finally finding our way back, seeking out and preserving where we can the fragments of natural beauty that remain.

One of the finest and rarest is the area in northern Florida where the traveler can still look down into the "mighty fountains" welling up from limestone springs, and drift through a place "as holy and enchanted / As e'er beneath a waning moon was haunted / By woman wailing for her demon-lover!" Though the demon-lover has, alas, gone the way of the heath hen and the Carolina paraquet, the enchantment is still there. On the clear "runs" where for miles one can see every inch of the river bottom; in the pinelands and hammocks and cypress swamps; on the lakes, and above all on that famous "black water" river, the Oklawaha — the Ockli-Waha, or Great River, as the Indians called it — one can recapture the sense of wonder that gives an almost religious quality to the writings of the early naturalists.

The Oklawaha is not a familiar river to most Americans today; less so, I imagine, than in the last century, when visitors from the north rhapsodized over the wonders of travel by excursion steamer on Florida's inland waters. Today's tourist, driving at eighty miles an hour through a billboard jungle, has little idea of the beauties that lie hidden in the softly rolling country between the harsh ribbons of cement. One of the most enchanting oases in this desert of progress is known as the "Marjorie Kinnan Rawlings country." It lies in north-central Florida, southeast of Gainesville (seat of the University) and east of Ocala and the north-south freeway. It is an area of rivers and lakes and crystal springs bubbling up from the underlying limestone aquifer known to geologists as the "Ocala dome" — the largest single water storage in the United States. It is a country of orange groves, hugging the lakes as insurance against frost; of stock farms with hundreds of acres of neatly fenced pasture, here and there shaded by great live oaks; of hardwood hammock (a few virgin stands remain); of pineland and scrub forest, famous for its abundance of game. The latter flourishes in the Ocala National Forest, an area approximately twenty by forty miles in extent, bordered by the St. Johns River on the east and the Oklawaha on the west. This scrub country is the scene of Mrs. Rawlings' novel *The Yearling;* west of the Oklawaha lies the town she made famous in *Cross Creek.*

The Oklawaha River itself rises in several large lakes near the center of the Florida peninsula. It flows north along the edge of the national forest and then turns abruptly eastward at Orange Springs to join the mighty St. Johns. A third of the way along its northward course it is swelled by the out-flow from that most fabulous of fountains, Silver Springs, which "with ceaseless turmoil seething / As if this earth in fast thick pants were breathing," pours forth some five hundred million gallons of water a day, so clear that the blue catfish on the bottom sixty feet below seem almost within arm's reach. Now commercialized and vulgarized, Silver Springs was at one time the mecca for travelers on the river-boats that made the trip upstream from Palatka, at the junction with the St. Johns.

Reading early accounts of this singularly scenic journey, one realizes how much we have lost, in purely aesthetic pleasure, by turning our backs upon our rivers. The old guidebooks give us the practical details. From Palatka to

Silver Springs, by Hart Line steamer, took twenty hours; the return trip only fifteen. (After experiencing this current in a canoe, I am surprised that the difference in time was not greater). The fare, in 1912, was seven dollars, "meals and berths included." It was an overnight trip, and the guidebook author waxes poetic when he describes, like many before him, the dramatic scene as darkness closes in: "A brazier forward on the upper deck is filled with pine roots and lighted, and the reflections of the leaping flames on the foliage and the water is indescribably weird and picturesque."

Sidney Lanier wrote the classic account of a trip on the Oklawaha in the opening chapter of his *Florida,* published

ten years after the close of the Civil War. Stricken with tuberculosis contracted in the Confederate Army, fated to die at the age of thirty-nine, the young poet wrote with a "passionate, hurrying eloquence." To him the Oklawaha was "the sweetest water-lane in the world, a lane which runs for more than a hundred and fifty miles of pure delight betwixt hedgerows of oaks and cypresses and palms and bays and magnolias and mosses and manifold vine-growths, a lane clean to travel along . . ." As the steamer wound its way upstream, the channel narrowed, "the blue of heaven disappeared, and the green of overleaning trees assumed its place. The lucent current lost all semblance of water. It was simply a distillation of many-shaded foliages, smoothly sweeping along beneath us." The mysterious shapes in the vine-clad forest formed a procession of poetic images in his mind, and finally, as darkness fell, "after this day of glory, came a night of glory . . . The stream which had been all day a baldrick of beauty, sometimes blue and sometimes green, now became a black band of mystery."

Lanier wrote almost a century ago. Like the side-wheelers on the Mississippi beloved by Mark Twain, like the canal boats and the Hudson River steamers, like a thousand other rivercraft that once combined leisurely travel with aesthetic enjoyment, the Oklawaha steamboats have long since vanished. Their hulks rot in the mud; their pine-knot flares will never be relit. Yet we can do better than simply look back on those early days with sad nostalgia. The attitude of the country toward our rivers has changed in recent years. Outdoor recreation has become a recognized need in an urban society. For the first time in our history, concern for the environment, for saving a fraction of our vanishing wilderness, is a popular cause and a political force. Given the wisdom and the strength, we have the means today of saving the Oklawaha and other wild rivers, of dedicating the finest of our still undammed and unpolluted waterways to purposes of adventure and creative enjoyment.

A master plan exists. In 1963 word came at last from Washington that we must make "adequate provision to keep at least a small stock of our rivers as we first knew them: wild and free-flowing — their numbers diminish as the recreational need for them grows. It takes but one harness to change a river's character forever." A presidential message reminded us that the time has indeed come "to identify and preserve free-flowing stretches of our great scenic rivers before growth and development make the beauty of the unspoiled waterway a memory." A special Wild Rivers Study Team, under the joint direction of the Secretaries of the Interior and Agriculture, recommended a Wild Rivers system under either state or federal administration. The first list of rivers included the "Oklawaha of Florida." The Study Team report of September 13, 1963, gives it top rating: "This river is of sufficient size and unique character and should be included in any system of wild rivers. It is felt that this use outweighs any other possible functions that have been proposed for the general area." The report goes on to mention the wealth and variety of the flora and fauna, the aquatic plant communities of particular ecological interest, the archaeological sites, and — *mirabile dictu* in present-day America — notes that "pollution is apparently nonexistent."

This was in 1963. What has happened? Midway in the

Study Team report lie two ominous sentences. "The United States Army Engineers' plans for a Cross-Florida Barge Canal includes the Oklawaha River. This will completely obliterate the study area in its present form by inundation of swamplands and bottom land habitat." Later on: "There are no plans to protect the river . . . Development by the U.S. Corps of Engineers of the Barge Canal is a definite threat to the mere existence of the stream." The same year that the Study Team's recommendation was published, the Corps of Engineers, whose pork-barrel appropriation bills are almost never voted down, got $5 million from Congress to begin work on the canal.

As the fatal impact of the project became evident, conservation organizations wrote in protest to the President, who had been so concerned that the beauty of the unspoiled waterway "might become only a memory." A typical reply came from the Bureau of the Budget: "The values of preserving the river in its natural state must be weighed against the benefits of developing a more economical transportation route. During the course of many years, congressional and other representatives of the State of Florida have strongly supported the Cross-Florida project. They must have seriously weighed the alternatives and decided that the benefits of the project outweighed the adverse impacts on the beauty of the river." They "must have" but they didn't. An alternative route which would have saved the Oklawaha was recommended by the conservationists; there is no evidence, however, that it was ever "seriously weighed." As for the "benefits" — benefits to whom? To a small group of shippers, to real estate speculators and other local business interests

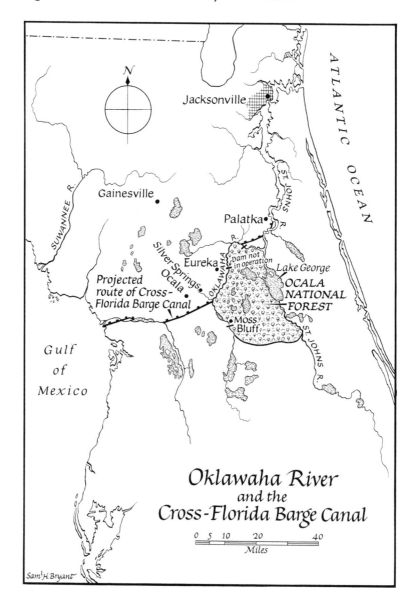

N

Jacksonville

ATLANTIC OCEAN

SUWANNEE R.

Gainesville

ST. JOHNS R.

Palatka

OKLAWAHA R.

Silver Springs

Eureka

Dam not in operation

Lake George

OCALA NATIONAL FOREST

Ocala

Projected route of Cross-Florida Barge Canal

Moss Bluff

ST. JOHNS R.

Gulf
of
Mexico

Oklawaha River
and the
Cross-Florida Barge Canal

0   5 10   20   40
Miles

Sam. H. Bryant

profiting from the taxpayers' money. The Oklawaha was scratched off the Wild Rivers list without a fight.

The idea of a canal across Florida is not new. It originated during the administration of Thomas Jefferson, as a means of eluding the pirates who roamed the West Indies, and of facilitating the transportation of mail from Washington to New Orleans. (Neither of these concerns is pressing today.) For over a century the scheme lay dormant; then during the depression of the thirties it was briefly but unsuccessfully revived as a make-work project. During World War II it was unearthed again as a means of protecting shipping from submarine attack, on the passage from the Atlantic to the Gulf. Studies had shown however that a "ship canal," deep enough to accommodate the draft of seagoing vessels, would raise havoc with the water table. But the Engineers now had a congressional authorization (passed in 1942) and they were not going to give it up. So they switched to a shallow "barge canal," and went ahead, proceeding under an authorization obtained more than twenty years earlier — voted during the war for a different purpose and at a time when almost no one realized how quickly our wilderness resources were going to disappear. And having picked a route that would destroy the river, having promised but failed to study alternatives, the Corps falsely claimed that it has no authority to change this route without a vote of Congress.

The route of the projected canal runs from Palatka on the St. Johns River to Yankeetown on the west coast. The impact of the western section on the Gulf coast's remaining wilderness is alarming, but the stretch we are concerned with here lies along the Oklawaha River valley upstream to Silver Springs — the classic scenic voyage of riverboats in times past. Two dams will completely kill this stretch: Rodman Dam near the mouth, already in operation, and Eureka Dam, built but not yet functioning, which will impound the river as far up as the Springs. In the circumstances, is the battle already lost? Must the canal be pushed ahead, despite the evidence that it will be (in the words of a leading biologist) "an environmental disaster"? The Secretary of State of Florida says that it must: "Both intelligence and, for those of you who wish, the Bible dictate that man is to have dominion over all the resources of the earth. Since most of us either believe in our own intelligence and/or in the Bible, let us be about the task of exerting our dominion over these resources." An admirably clear statement of the philosophy that is bringing our world to the brink of ruin.

Even in purely economic terms, the folly of the canal has been demonstrated again and again since its inception. When the project was reactivated in 1963, a former Army Engineer, using the Corps' own figures, showed that costs would far exceed so-called "benefits." Since then costs have gone up, and borrowing rates on money have soared. By the Corps' own admission, at the present long-term government interest rate the return on the investment today would be only 92 cents on the dollar. It is far less if one includes honest figures for weed control (estimated at about $8 million a year) and omits that imaginary asset, "recreation." The two are closely linked. Once the cool, fast-flowing Oklawaha has been turned into a series of warm, shallow lakes, nutrients accumulate and waterweeds take over. Poisoned, they rot on the bottom, taking oxygen from the water. In the words of the Game and Fresh Water Fish Commisson's report: "The eco-system which formerly supported high quality fishing, hunt-ing and aesthetic values is in jeopardy because the new system is a nutrient trap and functions similarly to a sewage treatment polishing pond." Recreation? No one who studies the balance sheet can disagree with Senator William Prox-mire's comment: "Pure blubber in the park barrel."

But we can't stop now, say the promoters, after so much money has already been spent. The same was said about the Everglades jetport. There a national park was threatened with extinction. Here it is a wild river valley which, under protection by the federal government, could become a superb wildlife sanctuary and recreational area. Much of the Okla-waha remains untouched. Even the lower stretch of the river will eventually recover if the water is released from Rodman Dam; wounds heal more quickly here than they do in north-ern climes. To get an impression of what is at stake, my wife and I decided to take a look for ourselves — first from the air and then, more slowly and intimately, on the surface of the river itself.

There is no vantage point like a low-flying plane for com-paring the works of God with the works of man. The drain-age of the Oklawaha is not, of course, a well-defined "valley" running between hills. Rather it is a mile-wide belt of mixed cypress and hardwoods; a deep green jungle, now in Novem-ber washed with pastel shades of red and purple and rusty brown. All but hidden by the tall trees except from directly overhead, the river — as one follows it downstream — is a meandering black thread, joined here and there by almost invisible tributaries, twisting and turning in ever wider loops as it approaches its mouth. Here, in the heart of Florida, lies an oasis of pure wilderness. As Marjorie Carr, one of the leaders in the fight to save the Oklawaha, has written: "The role the valley forest is serving, as a reservoir of wildlife for the adjacent lands, is most evident when seen from an airplane . . . To the west lie open pine lands, and the dry low forest of the Big Scrub spreads out to the east. Clearly, the valley forest serves as a safe highway and sanctuary for wildlife over an enormous area." Here, we learned, are found deer and bear, raccoon and otter and wildcat. And here are some of the finest flocks of that indicator of true wilderness, the wild turkey.

As we flew on downstream, we were suddenly jolted by the sight of the high white arc of a concrete bridge at the crossing of the Eureka road. Near the bridge rises the great mass of the Eureka Dam, still on dry land, waiting for the moment when the channel will be diverted and the last wild stretch of the valley will be drowned for ever.

Below Eureka lies a graphic history of how the wildest river can be broken and put between shafts. Dead water from the impoundment above Rodman Dam has replaced the running stream. A wide straight swath, its borders black against the forest edge, cuts the S curves of the river like the strokes of a dollar sign. This is the route of the still unfinished canal. More and more drowned trees, more and more waterweeds and debris; then the large expanse of the "reservoir" itself. The river has disappeared, though here and there its old channel can be detected, a green blanket of water hyacinths among the truncated trees. Scattered far and wide over the surface of the impoundment, looking from the air like handfuls of jackstraws, lie vast numbers of dead trees, some solitary, some in solid rafts. Crushed into the mud before the reservoir was flooded, they continue to float up through the ooze: gigantic corpses that refuse to lie quiet in their graves.

Though the scene from the air was bad enough, a close-up view was worse. The following day an outboard motorboat (no point in canoeing here) took us over the "Rodman Pool." We threaded our way among the floating snags, occasionally striking a sunken log with a jarring crash. In a thicket of standing trees, an airboat was drenching the carpet of hyacinths with poison, (2,4-D, mixed with fuel oil); the weeds in the open water had already been sprayed from helicopters. On a barge flying the ensign of the Army Engineers a crane was lifting one tree after another out of the water, piling them on an island to be burned. At the head of the reservoir, on the line of the future canal, stood the tree-crusher — or the "monster," as it is locally known — which had created such expensive havoc. Resembling an oversize tank, with a crossbar in front to knock down the living trees and two enormous tracks to crush them into the ground, it was an obscene symbol of man's war with the wilderness. We left the scene of carnage with relief. There still remained a long stretch of wild river. For the next two days we would explore it by canoe.

To launch one's canoe on a wilderness river is to realize a new dimension in space and time. A heavy morning mist was just burning off when we put in at Moss Bluff, the upstream limit of the free-flowing Oklawaha (there is a new dam just above). After the fall rains the water was high and the current strong; we were soon out of sight of human habitations, though not yet in wild country. We could hear a chain saw

cutting the slash pines that flourish in the sandy soil along the east bank; for some perverse reason the Ocala National Forest does not include the edge of the river which forms its boundary. To the west lay a flat pasture with a herd of beef cattle

accompanied by cattle egrets. A flock of killdeer, flying low upstream, split on either side of our canoe; phoebes darted over the water; scrub jays shrieked among the pines. The shores here were bright with the orange-red of the maples and deeper crimson of the sweetgum; glimpses of cardinals and mockingbirds and the song of a house wren suggested that we were still in open scrub country, as did the black vultures and turkey vultures wheeling far above us in the sky. Then to our delight a pair of sandhill cranes, recognizable at a distance by their outstretched necks and purposeful flight, flew directly overhead. For a moment we were back on the Yukon Flats in Alaska, another great nursery of birdlife that the Army Engineers would like to destroy with a needless dam.

As the river entered the true cypress swamp, its character changed. No longer did it have definable limits. Though the main channel was as clear as ever, the current ran not between banks of solid earth but through a winding avenue of trees knee-deep in the water. Instead of the occasional cypress tree standing alone, they extended far back from the river as far as the eye could reach through the tangled undergrowth, their boles arrow-straight, their branches hung with Spanish moss. Harriet Beecher Stowe wrote of them on the St. Johns River almost a century ago: "The long swaying draperies of the grey moss interpose everywhere their wavering outlines and pearl tints amid the brightness and bloom [she saw it in the spring] of the forest, giving to its deep recesses the mystery of grottoes hung with fanciful vegetable stalactites." As the brush country birds diminished, the waders became more abundant. One old cypress, heavily buttressed at the base, bare now but for delicate, feathery patches of russet needles, bloomed like a giant flower stalk with white blossoms of snowy and American egrets and the blue-gray of the great blue heron. Another was black with a canopy of boat-tailed grackles.

Compared to the bright flowering of spring, the autumn colors along the river were subdued, but they had their own subtle beauty: the head-high masses of pale purple asters climbing over the shrubs along the sunny edge of the channel, the dark shiny leaves of the magnolias, the red berries of the water holly leaning out over the river. All signs of civilization had vanished hours ago. The only sounds were the *plop* of a turtle as it dropped from its log, the squawk of a heron, and now and then a wave of mingled songbird chatter so loud and various as to remind us of the "dawn chorus" in a New England spring. And, of course, the woodpeckers. A common note in this forest is the loud *churr* of the (mis-named) red-bellied woodpecker, a bright little bird with zebra back and red crown, forever darting from one dead snag to another. But the great sight for the birdlover is the pileated. The "cock o' the woods" of New England is, accord-ing to Mrs. Rawlings, known at Cross Creek as the "Lord-God." "The woodpecker was enormous," she wrote, "swoop-ing from trunk to trunk of the orange trees, he appeared the size of a half-grown turkey. He was brilliant in black and red and white, and gave a loud clapper-like cry." This cry is the signature of the cypress swamp, as the weird quavering call of the loon is of the north woods.

Though even at high water there remain a few spots along the Oklawaha where one might pitch a tent, the nights in

November are too long for camping out. We made our trip in two stages, leaving a car at the end of each day's journey. By midafternoon of the first day we had reached the junction with Silver Springs, where Route 40 crosses the Oklawaha. Next morning we put in there for the somewhat longer run to Eureka, down the stretch of the river that will be wholly destroyed if the barge canal is ever finished.

After the previous day's experience, we feared an anticlimax, but we need not have worried. This "continuous river swamp or hydric hammock habitat," as a biologist describes it, is wilderness from start to finish: a self-contained world of water, trackless and inviting exploration, where even the casual canoeist (ignorant, as we were, of so much hidden life around us) cannot but share the sense of discovery that was felt by the first white men to see it, two centuries ago. We often put down our paddles to drift and watch. There was plenty to look at: an anhinga, or water-turkey — "the most preposterous bird within the range of ornithology" in Lanier's opinion — drying its outspread wings in the sun; an alligator stretched out on a log; a pair of buffleheads, most stylish black-and-white ducks, scampering ahead of our canoe like mergansers on a northern river; a barred owl that allowed us to drift silently beneath the low branch where he perched; a limpkin, oblivious to our presence a few feet away as he extracted a snail from its shell with his down-curved bill. "The Oklawaha," we read in *Cross Creek*, "is one of the two or three remaining haunts of the strange brown crane who cries before the rain."

The forest seemed ever more exotic and tropical, perhaps because of the abundance of tall cabbage palms and the spheres of mistletoe on the treetops. "Along the immediate edges of the stream," as Lanier noted from his steamboat, "every tree-trunk, sapling, stump, or other projecting coign of vantage is wrapped about with a close-growing vine." Bright green plumes of wild rice, with tiny yellow flowers, grew in the shallows. Here too were familiar butterflies: monarchs, tiger swallowtails, and the delicate, silver-spotted Gulf fritillary. As the river writhed in ever-growing oxbows, our main job was not so much to paddle ahead as to keep the canoe in the main channel, away from the swirling eddies and the occasional sawyer bobbing in the current. When we stopped to explore one of the side streams leading back into the swamp — which gave a sense of utter remoteness in a vast jungle — the main river on our return seemed like a highway.

Dusk was but an hour off when we reached Eureka. We pulled up our canoe below the high bridge spanning an expanse of dry sand, the bed of the future canal. Midway in the center span, a light had already been fixed to guide the

barges of tomorrow. On the light poles leading to the dam perched two red-shouldered hawks. Tracks of an otter marked the sand. Beside us flowed the river, dark and clear and free, as it had for a thousand years.

Must the Oklawaha, in the President's words, become only a "memory"? A year or two ago the answer might have been yes. Not so today. Thanks to that extraordinary group, Florida Defenders of the Environment, the public has been awakened to the crisis. The attempted rape of the Oklawaha has been denounced in the national press. The Department of the Interior would like to see it returned to the Wild Rivers system; the Forest Service is prepared to buy back the valley from the state and add it, as a recreation area, to the Ocala National Forest. A lawsuit, based on the people's right to save their environment, has been brought against the Army Engineers. The governor of Florida, after a long silence, is withholding his support of the canal pending further studies. In June 1970, the Secretary of the Interior asked the Army for a fifteen-month moratorium on construction while environmental costs and economic benefits can be evaluated. Meanwhile, a barge attempting to use the finished part of the canal at its western end became firmly stuck in the mud.

As of this writing, construction has virtually ceased. Eureka Dam remains high and dry; the tree-crushing monster lies rusting on the shore; and the river beloved by William Bartram and Sidney Lanier, though sorely injured, is still alive. Future generations may yet enjoy, as Coleridge wrote in his notebook, "some wilderness-plot, green and fountaineous and unviolated by Man."

— 8 —

The Golden Plains
of Tanzania

No SPOT ON EARTH is better suited than East Africa to dramatize the joys and the responsibilities of man's relation with the rest of the natural world: a world to which, for richer or for poorer, he is inevitably bound. It is a land of vast wealth, but of a kind that cannot be possessed. Indeed its unique asset, wildlife, exists by virtue of *not* being possessed. Though sadly diminished in numbers, the great mammals and brilliant birds of the African bush still present one of the world's major spectacles. Yet it is more than a spectacle. We sense an obligation not only to see but to understand. For in an age of triumphant technology, whatever we don't understand we sooner or later destroy.

In most of the so-called civilized world, destruction of the natural environment has almost reached the point of no return. Only in a few places like East Africa can one still experience, on a grand scale, the abundant life once found in so many parts of our planet. On the golden plains of Kenya and Tanzania, with their great herds of antelope — their giraffes and zebras and buffalo — an American sees as in a mirage our Great Plains in the days of Lewis and Clark: "This scenery already rich pleasing and beautiful was still further heightened by immense herds of Buffaloe, deer Elk and Antelopes which we saw in every direction feeding on the hills and plains." Watching the mixed herds of hoofed animals (of many more species than even primeval America knew), noticing the vegetation on which they feed (some of which looks wholly inedible), and studying the predators that in turn feed upon them, even the casual observer becomes aware of the close and complex relation of each animal to its environment. Here variety is not merely the spice but the condition of life. The fact is worth remembering, for it is a key to the problem of land use in a part of the world very different in its potential from the fertile areas of western Europe or America.

The problem of wildlife conservation in East Africa is obviously confined to no single region or country. Kenya, Uganda, and Tanzania can be considered an ecological unit. A giraffe cannot be expected to know when he crosses the invisible border between, say, the Mara Masai Game Reserve in Kenya and Tanzania's Serengeti National Park — nor, alas, when he crosses the equally invisible boundary of the park itself and the unprotected country where a poacher may be lying in wait to snare him and sell his tail for a fly whisk. But from the point of view of the American conservationist, one aspect of this vast subject that is of particular interest and immediacy is Tanzania's system of national parks and reserves, which — both figuratively and geographically — lie at the vital center.

Historically, there is a close link between the American

experience and the parks of Africa. When Colonel Stevenson-Hamilton was struggling back in 1905 to establish the great Kruger National Park he took courage from what had been accomplished here. "I had incidentally heard a good deal about the American national parks, and of their success as a public attraction. Would it conceivably be possible to wean the South African public from its present attitude towards the wild animals of its own country, which was that of regarding them either as a convenient source of exploitation, or as in incubus hindering the progress of civilization? . . . I sent for and read all the literature available concerning the American national parks, especially the Yellowstone, and was astonished at the vast amount of money which the U.S. Government thought it worth while to spend on it, and at the public enthusiasm displayed. The American public must surely be very different from ours!" Today, with American visitors to the East African parks outnumbering even the British, with American dollars helping to train African administrators, with our own national park system and universities cooperating in the training programs, the link has become stronger than ever.

Tanzania has five national parks. The oldest and greatest of these, the Serengeti, 5600 square miles in extent, lies south of the Kenya border (where it adjoins the Mara Masai Game Reserve), stretching from the vicinity of Lake Victoria in the west to Ngorongoro Crater and Olduvai Gorge (the site of Dr. Leakey's famous excavations) in the southeast. Lake Manyara National Park comprises about 125 square miles between Ngorongoro Crater and Arusha, the principal city of northern Tanzania, where the park administration is located.

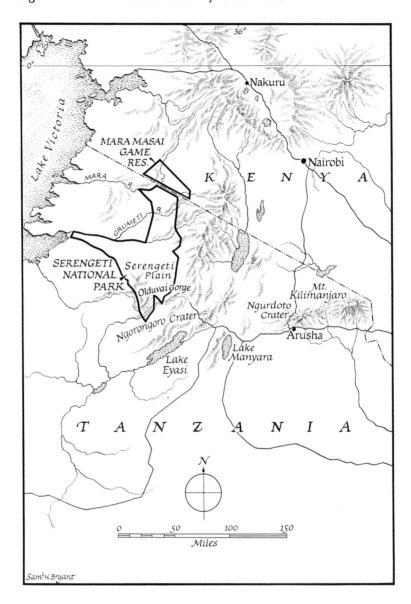

Sam'l H. Bryant

Ngurdoto Crater (not to be confused with Ngorongoro Crater, of which more later) is a little gem of 25 square miles near Kilimanjaro, where wildlife exists undisturbed by man. Finally, there are the two recently established national parks: Mikumi, near Dar-es-Salaam, and Ruana, a vast region bordering the Great Ruana River. All together, however, the parks make up a very small percentage of the country's land area; obviously a large proportion of the wild animals live outside the park limits. For their protection the Game Department administers a system of game reserves and controlled areas, allowing hunting safaris in the latter under strict regulations.

Though much slaughter in the name of sport has taken place in the past, legal hunting (as opposed to illegal poaching, which remains very serious) is no longer a principal threat to African wildlife. The dangers today are far more complicated and difficult to control than a game-hog with a high-powered rifle. So difficult, in fact, that pessimists believe Africa's great game herds to be inevitably doomed, as anachronisms in a modern world. Meanwhile, however, an increasing number of trained scientists and administrators are trying to weave a lifeline that will not simply save a handful of passengers but will hold the ship itself — Noah's Ark, if you will — off the rocks. This lifeline is composed of at least three principal strands. In the present state of uncertainty, they might best be phrased as questions: Can the needs of wildlife and native tribes be reconciled? Can the habitat itself be preserved? Do the new African governments care? With varying degrees of emphasis, these questions arise in every area where wildlife is at stake. I have arbitrarily chosen three lookout points from which to cast an amateur eye on questions that baffle even the experts, hoping that the impact of first awareness may compensate in some measure for lack of technical knowledge. Though I have selected these places because I happen to have visited them on safari with my family, there is also some logic in the choice. (1) Ngorongoro Crater, formerly a part of Serengeti Park, represents a pioneering attempt to reconcile the interests of wildlife and those of a pastoral people. (2) Serengeti Park itself is the largest — though still inadequate — completely protected wildlife habitat. (3) And, finally, at Lake Manyara one finds a good example of the type of native administration that does indeed concern itself with the future of Africa's wildlife.

Ngorongoro is the showcase of Tanzania. The crater of an extinct volcano 7600 feet above sea level, its slopes are heavily forested and its floor, 2000 feet or more below the rim and over 100 square miles in extent, is cool and well-watered compared to the nearby sun-baked plain. The first white man to lay eyes on it was the German explorer Oscar Baumann, on March 18, 1892: "At noon we suddenly found ourselves on the rim of a sheer cliff and looked down into the oblong bowl of Ngorongoro, the remains of an old crater. Its bottom was grassland, alive with a great number of game; the western part was occupied by a small lake." Next day he recorded: "The abundance of game was really magnificent. Large herds of antelope roamed around and long-maned gnus, light-footed zebras, and, singly or in pairs, appeared the broad backs of rhinos." Here also were the kraals of the pastoral Masai, though later the German colonial administration tried with some success to drive them out and two brothers named Siedentopf turned the whole crater into one fantastic farm and ranching operation, which — in addition to cattle — included the raising of ostriches and the taming of zebras. Under the British rule that followed World War I some Masai tribes returned, and they were well established when the area became — with the western Serengeti — a national park in 1940. Thereafter, conflicts between native rights and strict wildlife conservation were inevitable. In 1959 a solution was sought by excising 3000 square miles from the old Serengeti National Park to form the Ngorongoro Crater Conservation Area, to be managed for the joint benefit of the wild animals and the Masai who lived there.

Ngorongoro Crater has been described as a huge zoo, but the term is inept. A zoo implies restraint; the animals here are wild. Nor would the people who live among them take kindly to this description. To the visitor from outside, the resident Masai are more than a picturesque addition to the scene. They give it a meaning in human terms. I remember our first close-up view of the crater floor, as our Land-Rover twisted down the steep narrow road from the rim. It was late afternoon; the tawny plain and the pale blue, green-bordered lake were lighted like a stage. Hundreds of black dots moved slowly from right to left in snakelike lines; a denser pattern of heavier mottled shapes moved across midstage in the opposite direction, with a few slim upright figures in the rear. The first were wildebeests, or gnus, whose heavy-shouldered profile suggests at a distance our American bison; the second were Masai cattle and their herders, wending their way homeward to their corral within the village. Gray's *Elegy* in a new context; one could almost hear the curfew tolling the knell of parting day. Yet that clump of shade trees in the distance where we planned to pitch our tents were neither rugged elms nor yews; they were umbrella acacias and the fever trees familiar to Kipling's Elephant's Child. And no "rude fore-fathers" lay beneath them; since the Masai — with due re-gard for nature's cycle — lay out their dead on the open plain to be eaten by the hyenas.

The following evening we came to know these people a little better — or at least to get a sense of their way of life. It had been a long day, a kaleidoscope of sharp-edged new impressions. We had risen at dawn after a cold night, when a bank of mist still hung about the rim of the crater and hippos grunted from a grass-grown arm of the lake. Elephants were moving about in the fever trees near camp, and on the flat grassland beyond, where one loses all sense of perspective, a solitary wildebeest loomed up like some giant legendary creature. As we drove out onto the plain a hyena loped with his strange seesaw gait ahead of the Land-Rover and an owl flapped overhead on silent wings. A shallow pond, rimmed with white soda, was packed with red-billed ducks and their young; the delicate long-legged waders at the shoreline were avocets and black-winged stilts. The edge of the central lake itself was pink with flamingos. Circling it, we had stopped on a knoll near the site of the Siedentopfs' farm, whence the eye takes in the whole sweep of the crater floor, with its fabulous concentration of game; later we drove slowly among them to photograph a rhino and her child, to watch vultures and jackals fighting over a kill (probably made by a cheetah) and to tape-record the wildebeests' grunts and the zebras' high-pitched bark. Following an elephant track, we had entered an enchanted little valley of lush grass enclosed by over-arching fever trees, and surprised a pair of shy — and here quite rare — reedbuck. We had watched zebras knee-deep in the water drinking, with white egrets mounted sidewise like circus riders on their backs. And in exploring this Eden we had almost got shamefully stuck: soda flats look dry on top, but the deeper the wheels sink the wetter it gets, and even with our four-wheel drive we barely churned our way through. Back in camp by midday, we had spent the after-noon recording the monotonous but haunting songs of four young Masai warriors who had come to call. Now they had invited us to walk back with them as they drove their lowing herds of cattle to their village a mile away. We had become part of the scene that, the previous evening, we had watched from afar.

The sea of animals that encompassed us was a mixed and scrawny lot by American dairy-farm standards. In the Masai economy, however, where cows represent wealth and social status, numbers count, not butterfat content. In contrast, the guardians of this four-footed bankroll were a delight to look at. Slim, long-legged, the Masai has delicate features that show his Hamitic rather than Bantu origins. Until mar-riage, he cherishes an elaborate hairdo of clay-matted twists, parted fore-and-aft and stained with red ocher, while the enlarged lobes of his ears encompass a variety of wire and bead and ivory ornament. A blanket over one shoulder, a red cloth skirt, and of course the inevitable long-bladed spear, protection against lions. He has a smooth and rapid stride.

Within a few minutes the brown bulge on the plain toward which we were headed began to take shape: a group of low dome-shaped huts, built of mud and wattle, surrounding a corral fenced with brush. As we approached, a tiny boy began driving animals into the corral, among them a huge old bull whom he controlled with a small switch and great aplomb. The village patriarch rose to his feet, barely walking with the aid of two sticks; and a blind old man — straight out of the Old Testament — was sorting out a flock of sheep by touch. The girls now took over the milking, for which they use long hollow gourds, or kibuyus. We watched one

girl as she worked. The first few drops she poured back onto the ground, scattering it like a libation; one thought of Homer's Greeks pouring their wine to the gods. And while she milked one side of the cow, a calf was sucking on the other. Modern sanitary dairy farmers might question this procedure — including the rinsing of the kibuyus with cow urine — but to the visitor from a prepackaged, pasteurized world it was singularly refreshing. When the time came to race the sun back to camp, we were convinced that the crater would be a poorer place without the Masai.

Yet it will be an even poorer place if they abuse it. Pastoral people have played a dual and contradictory role in conservation. By fighting off the agricultural tribes, they have preserved the habitat of the wild animals among whom they live in mutual tolerance. A proud and warlike race, they keep poachers from living off the wild flesh that they themselves despise as food. But by overgrazing the range with their cattle — and worse with their sheep and goats — they have turned some areas of Masailand into near desert. Having already lost much of their ancestral territory to the pressures of settlement, they are naturally suspicious of any regulations to do with land. Here as elsewhere they do not always stick to their agreements: for example, their illegal clearing of the forest slopes could seriously endanger the water supply. Yet there are signs of rapport. The Masai who live in the crater have kept constant the number of villages and discouraged immigration from outside, even among their own people; the headman who formerly led the opposition to the Ngorongoro Crater Conservation Area has himself become an ardent conservationist. The Masai's special regard for the crater is understandable: over seventy years ago Baumann in his journal contrasted the healthy residents of Ngorongoro Crater with the starving people whom he found taking refuge in this elevated Eden from the drought-stricken plains below. Meanwhile the Masai are still there. Domesticated cattle and wild zebra may still be seen grazing side by side; domesticated tourists, if they act properly, will be received without condescension by a people whose unique charm is their indifference to our way of life.

· ·

In contrast to Ngorongoro Crater, which is a comparatively small and self-contained area, the Serengeti Plain is a vast grassland where, for the wildlife, mobility is a key factor in survival. As we plowed along the single road through the park, connecting the campground at Seronera with the crater, we felt at times like the only living creatures in an empty world. For miles in every direction stretched an unbroken expanse of sparse, sere grass, relieved here and there by one of those rocky outcroppings known as kopjes, rising like tiny islands of shade in a sun-drenched sea. On the far horizon, distorted by shimmering heat waves, a frieze of flat-topped acacias floated just above the plain. Lifeless? Not quite. Two, three dots against the pale blue sky. Another and another — perhaps a dozen now, circling, slowly descending, dots no longer, but the uptilted, splay-tipped wings of vultures settling in to a kill. Turning off the track, and taking our direction from the vultures, we came to a stop parked within a few yards of two heavily maned lions who were just finishing off a Thomson's gazelle, identifiable only by the short curved horns. One lion was obviously the senior partner; he had already had his fill. But the other was still at work. Growling as he ate, he would take a casual swipe at any vulture that ventured too close; when we turned off the motor in the Land-Rover we could hear the crunching of bones. There was little left for the vultures when these hunting companions finally rose lazily to their feet and strode off together, heads turning in unison like vaudeville actors on a stage, headed for a nearby kopje where they would sleep away the heat of the day.

Back on the road, we drove through another seemingly lifeless stretch and suddenly the plain came alive with antelope, shy ostriches stalking among them and watching us with uneasy alertness. Here evidently was preferred grazing, though the difference was not apparent to the untrained eye. Unfortunately we were not in the right place at the right time to witness the mass seasonal movements of wildebeest and other hoofed animals which so dramatically exemplify the importance of mobility in the life cycle of Africa's great mammals. For more than anything else, this migration underscores the inadequacy of the present limits of Serengeti National Park.

In 1959, as mentioned above, the Serengeti Park was cut in half; the eastern section, containing the crater highlands, became the Ngorongoro Crater Conservation Area, and a new section was added running north from Seronera to the Kenya border. This drastic move was made in recognition of the Masai's claim to grazing rights — which of course cannot be allowed in a national park. It was also based on the false assumption that the great wildebeest migrations would still be contained within the limits of the park. However, that same year there appeared in Germany Bernhard and Michael Grzimek's now famous *Serengeti Shall Not Die*, in which, on the basis of painstaking research from the air, they stated flatly: "We had now established that the huge herds of wildebeest, zebras and gazelles live outside the new borders of the Serengeti National Park for a large part of every year." Subsequent studies have confirmed the fact that the animals cross the western boundaries of the park during the dry season into unprotected country where they are subject to heavy poaching; again in the calving season herds of wildebeest will follow the fresh new grass across the eastern boundary to the foothills of the crater highlands and give birth to their young outside the park limits. Yet, as the Grzimeks point out, "The whole object of creating the Serengeti National Park was so that the last remaining great herds of grassland animals in Africa should be protected within its borders all the year round." For here is perhaps the last place in the world where great herds of ungulates — or hoofed animals — roam across the open range as did once the bison of the American West.

Estimates of the animal population of the Serengeti and adjacent Mara region of Kenya come to well over a million. That's a lot of animals. But we should beware of jumping to any complacent conclusions. If you know where to go for it, you can find local abundance of any species right up to the bitter end. Wildlife has already disappeared from most of the continent, much of it within our own lifetimes. As one authority writes: "Those who have not been privileged to see Africa's multitudes of wild animals in all their former grandeur have difficulty in visualizing how East Africa must have appeared half a century ago." Nor should one be deceived by the fact that there may be an *overpopulation* of certain species in certain areas, just as there is, for example, of elk in some of our national parks. It is an artificial situation, having to do with the needs of the animals in relation to the limited carrying capacity of the range. The visitor who returns from East Africa with wildebeest like spots before his eyes should not conclude therefore that the animals have it made.

The frequently drawn parallel between the African plains and the American West of a century ago also needs examination if it is not to mislead. One can fairly argue (in

an attempt to exorcise our guilt) that the great herds of American bison were doomed in any case; the choice was between them on the one hand and agriculture and beef cattle on the other. In most of East Africa, on the contrary, the climate, soil, and resulting vegetation are suitable *only* for mixed species of wild game. Rainfall is sparse and uncertain. By agricultural standards the soil is poor. The grass cover is fragile; overgrazing by cattle or sheep, combined with a period of drought, can reduce it to dust, at the same time encouraging other plants to invade the grasslands. Yet country like this, when undisturbed, can support large numbers of wild animals because over aeons of time each species has evolved in such a way as to find its own ecological niche. Whereas in a herd of cattle each cow is competing with its neighbor for the same blade of grass, in a mixed herd of wild animals the different species utilize the various grasses, shrubs, and trees which are growing together in the same area. As the well-known ecologist Lee M. Talbot has written: "Food preferences of these wild ungulates are to a large degree complementary to each other and the plant species preferred are often those unpalatable to domestic livestock." (Experiments indicate that various species of wild game may produce three to seven times as much meat per square mile of grazing land as domestic cattle — an important factor in deciding the most economic use of land outside the parks.) There is still much that we do not understand about the seasonal migrations, population dynamics, distribution of rainfall, the carrying capacity of the range. The Serengeti Research Project, currently being conducted by a group of leading ecologists and game biologists, is of importance not only to the future of the Serengeti itself but to conservation throughout East Africa.

Four days before he reached Ngorongoro Crater, Dr. Baumann had recorded in his journal the first impact of another spectacular scene. The expedition had made the exhausting climb up the Rift wall: "When, after a strenuous ascent, we arrived at the magnificent plateau, it was almost evening. There, on the top, a wonderful view over the shimmering Lake Manyara compensated us for our efforts . . . Cool, clean air refreshed us, at this height clear streams rushed between slopes covered with fine grass; a dark forested mountain range appeared to the north." Today's traveler to Lake Manyara National Park sees much the same prospect from the top of the escarpment, though in our case the Land-Rover had done all the work. Descending to the level of the lake, we stopped for supplies at the village of Mto-wa-Nbu (River of Mosquitoes), whose main street was less a street than an international bazaar, with everything laid out for sale from tiny piles of coffee beans and finely woven baskets to bunches of ripe bananas and huge bundles of sugar cane. Here we met the park warden, an enthusiastic and intelligent African whose authority seemed to extend beyond his official duties: he casually broke up a fistfight in the crowd while scarcely interrupting his conversation with us. The warden spoke modestly, but he was working at the true heart of the conservation problem — which is, of course, education. The visitor from abroad realizes with something of a shock that many Africans in the towns go through life without ever seeing an elephant or a rhino or a buffalo. And though the animals figure so permanently in their folklore, the native attitude is, quite naturally, to consider them as a menace to herds or crops or as a source of meat. It is well expressed by a native Kenyan who, after studying in the United States, returned to East Africa to make a career of game management and conservation: "In 1948 I started schooling, and in our first reader was a story of how a lion had devastated an area not too far from our school, killing people and cattle, and of how the invader had been ultimately killed to save the rest of the people. Other wild game . . . used to invade gardens in great numbers . . . To encourage hunting, the people who had killed the truly fierce animals, such as lions, or the big animals, such as elephants, received special recognition. This enhanced their social status, especially with women. As a result, people in my age group have grown up in an area deprived of the natural beauty and richness of much of our wildlife."

To the race-conscious African, moreover, the wild animals represent a past that he wants to forget, when his country was exploited as the white man's playground: if it's the animals they want, we'll kill them off and they will leave us alone. The national parks, concerned with saving the animals, were looked at with suspicion. "Because the Parks were used almost exclusively by Europeans," writes John S. Owen, director of Tanzania national parks, "they were regarded as being run exclusively in the interests of the white man." The job for the immediate future is "not only to awaken public opinion but to change it." A huge task. The warden here at Manyara gave us an example of how the park authorities, with help from many sources, are going about it. One of his best tools is a wildlife film, with narration in Swahili, made by a young American who was for two years education officer of the Tanzania national parks. Africans of all ages come for miles to see it. It is one example of the educational information program which is being steadily extended through the use of films directed to African audiences, showing the purpose and value of the national parks. Posters in Swahili carry the words: "Our National Parks are the envy of the world — be proud of them." "Our National Parks bring good money into Tanzania — preserve them." Pride and profit. At the moment, both are essential. The former without the latter is hardly sufficient in a new and struggling economy. It speaks well for the Tanzanian government that it has contributed generously from its small budget to support the parks, recognizing a duty to the world to preserve this unique heritage, and confident that as tourism continues to increase it will become the nation's greatest industry. Soon after achieving independence, the government promised, "We will do everything in our power to make sure that our children's grandchildren will be able to enjoy this rich and precious inheritance of wildlife."

There is a good deal more to running a park or natural reserve than building a few roads and campgrounds. In East Africa particularly, a technical knowledge of game management is essential. Hence the great significance of the College of African Wildlife Management, established in 1963 at Moshi near Kilimanjaro under the auspices of an American organization, the African Wildlife Leadership Foundation. Here come African students from the game departments and national park services of Tanzania, Kenya, and Uganda, on a two-year course in such subjects as wildlife ecology, population dynamics, range management, and conservation in all its manifold aspects. Their studies are less from books than in the field. The library-bound college student in America might view with envy this paragraph in the monthly newsletter from Moshi: "Exploratory journeys were made over a large part of the Reserve, combining anti-poacher patrols with instruction on the ecology of the area . . . Three cadets had a remarkable experience on one line-abreast sweep: they met a group of 45 lions. On this occasion the behaviour of the cadets and the lions was exemplary." These students take their instruction where they find it, and it doesn't always

come from a Doctor of Philosophy: "Following the sighting of a new bush fire an immediate search led to the capture of an Ndorobo poacher. He was an old man who was still following the traditional hunting and honey-gathering life of his tribe and as no useful purpose would have been served by prosecuting him, he was returned to his home area where the Chief agreed to keep an eye on him. Some of the excellent bush skills which were demonstrated by this Ndorobo were very instructive, particularly his ability to make fire." The safari moved on to Lake Manyara, where they explored the "magnificent ground-water forest" and studied the "great variety and abundance of birdlife" for which Lake Manyara is famous.

Reading this report takes me back to our own brief visit to the area. After the warden had shown us the small interpretive museum at the park gatehouse, we drove slowly through a lush and infinitely varied forest, on a dirt road overarched by enormous fig trees from which families of baboons would descend en masse to watch us from a patch of sunlight before bounding into the darkness. Elephants were all about, in small groups and large herds. One young male blocked our passage on what he clearly considered his road; we didn't argue, and all he did was trumpet loudly as we finally slipped past. Back at the lake shore by evening, we camped on the dry saline flats between the water's edge and a scrubby plain studded with great baobab trees which could have been imagined only by an African god or Arthur Rackham. Just before nightfall — which comes with startling suddenness in the tropics — we heard a rumbling overhead that might have been a distant jet plane. Flying into the sunset were hundreds of flamingos, not in a V like geese but in a perfect arc, a scimitar slicing the sky. The roar of their wings spoke louder than words of the wild beauty that such a park as Manyara holds in trust for the world.

The fact that the future of Africa's wildlife is the world's business is now generally recognized. The IUCN (International Union for the Conservation of Nature) and the World Wildlife Fund put major emphasis on threatened African species. Programs for conservation and game management, which were a British responsibility during the colonial period, now receive strong support from the United States. As the park system develops, the objective is more and more to bring the Africans themselves into the parks, which will be their responsibility in the future. This future, however, remains a world concern. Here the decision will be made whether our greatest animals live on in the wild or are relegated to zoos or to extinction. "Any man's death diminishes me," wrote John Donne, "because I am involved in mankind . . ." So those of us who recognize man's kinship with wild nature are diminished whenever, through man's agency, another form of life becomes extinct. In the present century, the bell tolls on the average of once a year for some species of mammal. Hope lies in the fact that it no longer tolls unheard.

— 9 —

The Rhinoceros
at Bay

I N ALL THE ANNALS of conservation, one could scarcely find a more poignant or more bizarre chapter than the battle to save the rhinoceros. The rhino is the embodiment of wildness, a living link between our world and the world of the distant past. His ancestry can be traced far back into the Tertiary period, before the Ice Age, long before the emergence of man. Yet within a comparatively few years, his very existence has become threatened. A formidable creature, with few natural enemies in the wild, he has been peculiarly vulnerable to man's weapons. Needing space around him, he has suffered severely from the shrinking of his habitat. Worst of all, this "living fossil" is the victim of a superstition which is itself a relic of the Dark Ages.

Of all creatures on earth, the rhinoceros appears at first glance the least likely to be associated with the art of love. The great horn that decorates his nose, and from which his name is derived, is not generally considered an object of beauty or endearment. Yet the belief in this horn's aphrodisiac and other magical properties has existed for countless centuries. And incredible as the fact may seem, the persistence of this belief down to our own day is a deadly threat to the comparatively few rhinos left on earth.

In the story of the rhino one can see a head-on collision of modern science and ancient myth. As conservationists have learned to their sorrow, some myths die hard. For instance, many otherwise rational persons still think in terms of "good animals" and "bad animals"; they cherish the dove and the deer, they hate the hawk and the wolf. With the rhinoceros the situation is more complicated. He is neither loved nor hated; but he has been senselessly persecuted and misunderstood. Few people know, or care, about his present predicament. They scarcely even realize that he comes in various shapes and sizes, some of which may soon be permanently off the market. Of the many types of rhinoceros that once walked the earth — including the woolly rhino that was a contemporary of the mammoth — five species have lasted until today: two in Africa, and three in Asia. When we think of rhinos, the picture that flashes on the mind's eye is almost always that of the black rhinoceros of the African bush (*Diceros bicornis*), prize subject for every photographic safari (anyone can get a chilling shot of a rhino's "charge" from the safety of a moving Land-Rover) and, in African wildlife films, the shortsighted old curmudgeon who provides artistic contrast to the light-footed, frolicking gazelles. Far less known is the African white or square-lipped rhinoceros (*Ceratotherium simum*), recently rescued from the verge of extinction. And few people indeed have seen all three of the Asian species: the great Indian or one-horned rhinoceros (*Rhinoceros unicornis*), now surviving precariously in Nepal and Assam in northeastern India; the Javan (*Rhinoceros sondaicus*) and the Sumatran (*Dicerorhizus sumatrensis*), both of which have all but disappeared.

To understand the rhinos' situation today, to take practical means that they shall not perish from the earth — leaving it so much the poorer — we must turn back upstream to the days of Marco Polo and Europe's first contact with Cathay. It is a tortuous voyage, full of cross currents and dark whirlpools where myth and science join and separate and join again. The object of the search is the most treasured animal of the medieval world; the most treasured and necessarily the most elusive, since its value depended on the fact that it did not exist.

The unicorn that faces the lion on the British coat of arms, or the delicate prancing creature of "The Hunt of the Unicorn" tapestries, seems about as remote from a rhinoceros as a butterfly from a caterpillar — and is, in fact, as close. Years ago Odell Shepard showed in his *Lore of the Unicorn* how distorted descriptions of the rhinoceros, blended with features of other animals such as that long-horned antelope, the oryx, recounted by travelers and preserved in bestiaries, lay at the back of the unicorn legend. Aelian, a third-century Roman writer, repeats from hearsay that "there are mountains in the interior of India which are inaccessible to men and therefore full of wild beasts. Among these is the unicorn" — and goes on to describe an animal which has the mane of a horse, the feet of an elephant, and the tail of a goat, with "a single black horn" between its brows, an animal of "great strength of body" and solitary habits. A strange compound, but obviously more rhinoceros than anything else. By the

Middle Ages, the connection is taken for granted. Describing Lesser Java (now Sumatra), one of the remote kingdoms of the great Khan, Marco Polo writes: "They have wild elephants and plenty of unicorns, which are scarcely smaller than elephants. They have the hair of a buffalo and feet like an elephant's. They have a single large, black horn in the middle of the forehead . . . They have a head like a wild boar's and always carry it stooped towards the ground. They spend their time by preference wallowing in mud and slime. They are very ugly brutes to look at. They are not at all such as we describe them when we relate that they let themselves be captured by virgins, but clean contrary to our notions." This is a fair description of the Sumatran rhinoceros, which in youth at least is somewhat hairy. The business of capture by virgins — who do not seem per se the ideal choice for such rough work — is baffling unless one is familiar with the approved method of hunting the unicorn. The technique is described in Richard de Fournival's *Bestiare d'Amour:* "For this is the nature of the unicorn, that no other beast is so hard to capture, and he has one horn on his nose which no armour can withstand, so that no one dares to go forth against him except a virgin girl . . . Therefore wise huntsmen who know his nature set a virgin in his way; he falls asleep in her lap; and while he sleeps the hunters, who would not dare to approach him when awake, come up and kill him." An unsportsmanlike procedure, but in a field where anything is fair. For we are dealing here less with the chase than with that other blood-sport, the art of love.

The valuable part of the unicorn was of course the horn. In days when poisoning was an accepted method of political advancement, the well-known fact that a unicorn horn would sweat or change color in the presence of poison made it a useful adjunct to a banquet table. Up to the sixteenth century physicians prescribed powdered unicorn horn "as a cure for all poisons, for fevers, for bites of mad dogs and scorpions, for falling sickness, worms, fluxes, loss of memory, the plague, and prolongation of youth." Most of these uses are now obsolete. It is the "prolongation of youth" that persists. One has only to substitute the rhino's horn for the unicorn's — as was in fact often done during the Middle Ages — to realize the ancient origins of the present threat to the rhino's survival.

Unicorn horns, or "alicorns," were kings' treasures. Benvenuto Cellini tells of one that Pope Clement VII presented to Francis I on the marriage of the Pope's niece, Catherine de Médicis, to his son. Up to the time of their civil war, the English treasured the "Horn of Windsor," which once belonged to Queen Elizabeth I. According to Hakluyt, this fine horn was picked up on an island in Frobisher's Strait in the Arctic. The story rings true, since the alicorn of medieval Europe — the straight, sharp, spiral horn of the unicorn tapestries — was in actuality the single spearlike tusk of that arctic member of the whale family, the narwhal. The equally real, if less beautiful, horn of the rhino entered Europe from the opposite direction, through the growing trade with the Indies. Like unicorn horn, rhino horn was carved into drinking cups to safeguard against poison, as it still is in Nepal and parts of India. (A beaker used by Rudolf II of Germany in the sixteenth century is preserved in the Copenhagen Museum.) In the form of a powder, it was also used as an antidote for all ills, including impotence. Eventually however, with the coming of the age of reason and the advent of modern medicine, the bottom fell out of the market for rhino horn in the Western world. In the East, on the contrary, it is literally worth its weight in gold.

A creation of man's imagination, the unicorn is immortal. Is his living prototype doomed to disappear through man's agency, after existing for millions of years? The rhino has become a symbol of an almost lost world. Fearful of aspect, solitary by nature, he precariously holds his own in parts of Africa and Asia: the two continents on which the great beasts of the past have not wholly succumbed to advancing civilization. Making his acquaintance, however casually, has its special rewards. As we look back at the recent history of the two African and the three Asian rhinos, we become blindingly aware of how many facets there are to the complex problem of wildlife conservation.

To those who have lived and worked with rhinos, I apologize in advance for the occasional use of the first person. Even the most fleeting experience has more life than a statistic. Some would argue, of course, that a biographer should never meet his subject at all, lest he be seduced by the latter's charm. Here I plead guilty from the start.

The first rhinoceros I ever met outside a zoo was seven months old, no larger than a medium-sized pig, and utterly charming. He was a black African rhino and belonged to Nick Carter, a former game scout then living at Kiboko (Swahili for "hippopotamus") in Kenya. Kiboko is a sort of oasis on the long dry road from Nairobi to Mombasa, and is famous as the home of late great J. B. Hunter, one of the last

of Africa's old-time "white hunters." The baby's name was Little Owl; he had been adopted by Nick when his mother was killed by poachers. Though for obvious reasons he was not given the run of the house, he achieved the same end by pushing down, like a miniature bulldozer, any barrier that was put in his way. Highly sociable, he could not bear to have Nick out of his sight. Toward guests he was as friendly as a puppy, but more dignified.

Behind the house were three heavy stockades. One was empty; the other two each contained a full-grown wild rhino: a male and a pregnant female. Nick's self-appointed task, which had made him known throughout East Africa, was to transfer the remaining animals from unprotected areas such as the one we were in, where they were being poached for their horns, to the safety of the national parks. Through great courage and persistence, aided by a trained staff of Kikuyu hunters, he had perfected a unique means of hunting rhinos. His weapon was a homemade crossbow shooting darts loaded with anaesthetic. A dart in the rump would knock the beast out for a brief period, during which it was bound, loaded onto a truck by means of winch and rollers, and transferred to one of the stockades. Here it was examined and treated for any injuries or disease, then transported by truck to a national park and released. In summary it sounds simple. It wasn't.

I never saw Nick capture a rhino, though we had one good morning's hunt. We were up at six. Half the party rode in a Land-Rover whose front fender had been crumpled by a beleaguered rhino some weeks earlier. The other half rode in the truck, looking, in Nick's words, "like aristocrats in a tumbril." Crash helmets were *de rigueur* for both. As the Land-Rover turned off the "track" into the bush, I could see why. It was rough country, mostly grassland and scattered scrub, thickets of thorn trees and an occasional huge baobab standing apart in grotesque splendor. The place was full of game. Flocks of yellow-legged partridge flushed ahead of us, red-billed hornbills flapped heavily by, warthogs with flaglike tails erect paraded into the bush, and a herd of zebra galloped parallel to our course, raising a red dust against the rising sun. As we approached a shy, solitary oryx, I was reminded of the unicorn. One can well understand how his spearlike horns, seen at a distance by a credulous observer, might be taken for a single horn springing from the forehead. The Arabian oryx, which once ranged through much of the Near East, is doubtless a secondary source of the unicorn legend. Indeed his graceful body is much closer to representations of that mythical creature than the great hulk of the rhinoceros, and his lovely head is a far likelier burden for a maiden's lap.

Bouncing through the bush, we found fresh rhino sign, but no rhino. We did find a Volkswagen belonging to poachers, cleverly concealed in the underbrush. (Our Kikuyu hunters deflated the tires and removed the timer, hoping to cause some embarrassment when the next quick getaway was in order.) Farther along, a lioness leapt across our bows. Then a Very light went up from the truck, by now a mile or more away. They had sighted a rhino. After a brief exchange on the walkie-talkie, we raced to join them. When we arrived, the beast had disappeared, but his tracks were easy to follow through the light ash of a burned-over stretch of grassland. Two Kikuyu trackers, keen and graceful as bird dogs, jogged ahead of the Land-Rover. Then abruptly the burned area ended, the tracks faded away into concealing grass. We kept on hopefully and once, at the glimpse of a dark shape, Nick readied his crossbow. But it turned out to be an ostrich. By now the sun was high and we reluctantly headed back to Kiboko, our disappointment lightened by the sight of a whole herd of oryx and, as we approached the river, a statuesque group of waterbuck. Nick would catch up with the rhino another day.

Though concerned specifically with the black rhinoceros, Nick Carter's operation involved important principles and techniques applicable to other threatened species. Specimens of the rare Hunter's antelope, for example, have been captured in Kenya's Northern Frontier District, where political turmoil makes protection all but impossible, and released in the game parks of the south. Most spectacular was the recent project to save the Arabian oryx. Ruthless hunting with jeeps and Tommy guns had reduced this beautiful animal from its former abundance to about two hundred individuals scattered throughout the desert. A team of experts successfully pursued and roped six of them, and flew them to Phoenix, Arizona. In a large enclosure, together with individuals contributed from zoos, they have thrived and bred; the future of the species seems secure.

As late as 1900 the black rhino was to be found throughout all of Africa south of the Sahara, excluding only the rain forests of West Africa and the Congo. A traveler wrote at the turn of the century: "From all sportsmen and prospectors who have visited out-of-the-way districts I have heard the same story of the great number of these fine old beasts." The rhino's tough hide was a protection against primitive native weapons. But not against the modern high-powered rifle. He was killed off as a nuisance in the neighborhood of settlements and he was slaughtered in the name of sport. The trade in horns was staggering. An early official report states, "Last quarter three thousand pounds weight of rhino horn passed through the Customs at Mombasa in transit from Kilima Njaro." Today the rhinos' only chance for survival is within the national parks and wildlife reserves. Their decline may be a major factor in the change of the habitat itself. By feeding on coarse and prickly vegetation, they have probably helped to maintain the equilibrium between bush and open grassland in semiarid areas. Such are the interconnections in the seamless web of life.

The web of superstition is even more far-reaching and complex. Shift the scene to a hole-in-the-wall druggist's shop in

Taipei, capital of Formosa. There, in December 1965, I saw
the sordid last act of a tragedy that had begun with death
somewhere in the African bush. In the shop's showcase was
a weird assortment of supposed aphrodisiacs. There was
ginseng root, which the Chinese have accepted as a substitute for the vanishing mandrake ("Go, and catch a falling
star, / Get with child a mandrake root"). There were antlers
and dried sexual organs of a deer. And in the center display
case was the unmistakable horn of an African black rhino,
for sale at $75 an ounce. (The current price is said to be
$200 an ounce or more.) Though scientific analysis of the
horn has shown that its ingestion cannot, except in the imagination, have any rejuvenating effect, this is of little concern
to the poacher who makes a fortune from a single kill. In
Hong Kong the trade is equally brisk. Unfortunately the
rhino, of all animals, is most vulnerable to poaching pressure.
Like the elephant, it has a low rate of reproduction; only the

DREAM OF UNICORNS *by John Wesley*

longevity of the individual enables the species to survive. And so long as the myth of the horn's magic power endures, only strict policing at the source can save it.

The history of the other African species, the white or square-lipped rhinoceros, is parallel to that of the black rhino, though in some ways it is both more shocking and more encouraging. The "white" rhino, incidentally, is gray, not white. Its name comes from *weit*, Afrikaans for "wide," and refers to its great square muzzle; it is a grazer not a browser. Scientifically, it is divided into two subspecies: an isolated northern population in the Sudan (well known to the ancient world) and the more familiar, and once so abundant, subspecies of the south.

Almost as heavy as a hippopotamus, the white rhino is twice the size of the black, but much gentler. Indeed, one naturalist who knows the species well finds that on close acquaintance it "seems so helpless and confused that one feels inclined to comfort this huge pachyderm." This approachability, together with its habit (unique among the rhino tribe) of grazing in groups in open grassland, made the white rhino peculiarly vulnerable. To the well-armed hunter it was easy game, and profitable. It was taken not only for its horn but for its hide — which was prized for making whips — and for its tasty flesh. The parallel to our own American bison is obvious. In both cases a species was virtually wiped out, and then rescued at the last possible moment. If anything, the rhino story, to which new chapters are being added every year, is the more dramatic.

First described in the early nineteenth century, the southern race of the white rhino was then to be found throughout South Africa. Its decline began shortly thereafter, with the coming of firearms in the hands of European hunters. As late as 1871 it was reported still numerous in uninhabited parts of Transvaal, in Southern Rhodesia, and in the southern part of Mozambique. About that time, the wholesale slaughter began. Two white hunters, for example, recorded killing 80 rhinos in a single season. A European trader in Southern Rhodesia, employing some 400 native hunters, all but exterminated the rhinos in his territory. By the nineties, the species was considered practically extinct; as with our buffalo, only bleached skulls remained to indicate its former range. Then in 1897, just before it would have disappeared forever from the earth, two game reserves were established in Natal. Henceforth, the figures tell the story. In 1920 the estimated number of white rhinos was 20. In 1929, 120. In 1932, 220. In 1959, 600. Today there are more animals than the two small reserves can support. In a spectacular program of live transportation, rhinos are being shipped to game reserves throughout Africa, as well as to zoos in other parts of the world. Kruger National Park received 90 rhinos in 1964. During the same year, in a reserve in Transvaal, occurred a momentous birth: the first white rhino to be born outside Natal in seventy years!

We speak of a "brush with death"; here is a "brush with extinction" to make the conservationist shudder, but also to give him heart. It shows that no such situation is entirely hopeless when modern scientific knowledge and strict enforcement of the law are brought into play.

· ·

The rescue of the African white rhino is one example of what can be done when we care enough to do it. Preservation of African wildlife has, in recent years, become a world concern. But what of Asia, the other continent that still harbors remnants of the world's great tropical fauna? Short of a miracle, two of the three Asian species seem doomed. The Sumatran, smallest of living rhinos, was formerly found throughout Southeast Asia. As late as the 1920s they were abundant in the Mekong Valley, and hunted in the vicinity of Saigon. Today a few individuals survive in widely scattered parts of their former range; the largest "pocket," recently estimated at a minimum of 28 animals, is in a wildlife reserve in Sumatra. Some of the rhino's favorite habitat has become a battlefield; everywhere persecution continues to the end. When a rhino is sighted, it is generally tracked to its death. There are well-attested stories of one Chinese trader in Sumatra who had a standing order of $2500 for a large horn, another who was offering a new American car for a whole carcass — since the blood and various organs are also considered medicinal. One almost yearns for the old days of absolutism, when a trader in the East Indies sent commodities to the King of Junsaloam, off the Strait of Malacca, "to barter for Ambergriese and for the hornes of Abath [rhinoceros] whereof the King only hath the traffique in his hands."

The Javan rhinoceros, a close relative of the great Indian, is gone from its once extensive range on the mainland. An estimated two dozen to four dozen individuals maintain a precarious existence in the Udjung Kulon Reserve, a peninsula at the westernmost tip of the island. The exploding human population, with its needs for agricultural land, has all but squeezed them out. That they exist at all is probably due to an incident unique in the annals of conservation, which is not without its grim humor. Immediately after the last war, when the Japanese guards for the reserve had been withdrawn and not yet replaced by the Indonesian government, a famous Chinese poacher entered the reserve to kill the last of the rhinos for their horns. However, he was promptly killed himself by a still rarer animal, the Javan tiger. Thus other poachers were frightened off, receiving little sympathy from the native residents, who believe the tigers to be the souls of their departed ancestors. One vanishing species had unwittingly saved the other.

"I went to see the Rhinoceros or Unicorn," wrote John Evelyn in his diary for October 22, 1684, "being the first I suppose was ever brought to England." It was a great Indian rhinoceros — the only Asian species most of us can hope to see today. A live rhino had appeared in western Europe almost two centuries earlier, shipped from Goa, on the western coast of India, around the Horn to Lisbon; and some years later another was sent as a present to the King of Portugal. A sketch of this animal — plus a large dose of artistic imagination — was the source for Albrecht Dürer's well-known engraving. This engraving is referred to scornfully in an eighteenth-century illustrated natural history, *Bruce's Travels:* "It was wonderfully ill executed in all its parts, and was the origin of all the monstrous forms under which that animal has been painted, ever since, in all parts of the world."

In those days the rhino flourished over a large part of

northern India as far west as the Indian Ocean, and north to Kashmir. But as wilderness gave way to cultivation, the Indian rhino's Lebensraum shrank to a few pinpoints on the map. An estimated 600 animals survive, most of them in sanctuaries in Nepal and in the Kaziranga Wildlife Sanctuary in Assam. My wife and I visited Kaziranga several winters ago, in the company of the former assistant director of the national parks of Rhodesia, who was already intimately acquainted with the two African species.

Has any park in the world such a dramatic approach? From Calcutta, your plane flies due north (to avoid East Pakistan) toward Kanchenjunga, its snow-covered massif dazzling white in the early morning sun. Westward rises the summit of Everest. A right-angle turn and the course lies along the broad Brahmaputra Valley. Everywhere the brown earth is under cultivation, in rice paddies or tea gardens stretching to the horizon. Then directly below appears a green oasis of tall grass and swamp and luxuriant forest

cover. This is Kaziranga. Some twenty-five miles long and eight miles wide, it lies along the south bank of the river. In a few minutes one has flown over it, en route to the nearest airport fifty miles beyond. But from a naturalist's point of view, this is one of the most important spots in all of eastern Asia.

A swampy and virtually trackless area, Kaziranga can be explored only from elephant back — which we found far superior to a Land-Rover or jeep: one feels a part of the landscape rather than an intrusion upon it. The magic hour is just after dawn. When we arose that first chill morning, a full moon hung on the western horizon. By the time we had mounted our elephant the stars had faded and there was enough light to ford the shallow river near the entrance to the refuge. Guided by the mahout (who sits on the animal's neck with his bare feet behind the ears) our mount pitched and rolled as his feet sank deep in the mud of the river bottom; then he scrambled up the far bank and plunged into elephant grass that rose above our heads, dripping with dew. The heavy morning mist gave every object a two-dimensional quality. Individual trees stood out in delicate silhouette; when a white egret alighted in the topmost branch of an acacia, one had the momentary illusion of an ink-wash painting from the brush of a Chinese master.

From somewhere in the swamp at our back came the trumpeting of a wild elephant. Our elephant replied, and we took up the trail, finally coming on four black backs, humping up like whales in the sea of grass. The largest was a full-grown female who made a noisy but token charge at these intruders on her privacy; the smallest, a tiny calf, whose scars from a recent attack by a tiger explained his mother's touchiness.

Leaving the family in peace, we entered a broad swale of close-cropped grass, at the center of which lay a shallow blue lake or *bil*, almost choked with water hyacinths. As the mist thinned, a group of dark gray shapes became a herd of wild water buffalo, including one old bull with a huge spread of horns. The doglike figures scampering through the short grass were hog deer; farther off, shapely swamp deer watched us with more curiosity than fear, and a wild pig trotted along the edge of the lake. Suddenly, without warning, we came on our first rhino. Two-thirds down in a mud wallow, he loomed out of the fog like a ship at sea. As he clambered out on the drier ground the illusion was strengthened by his coloring: battleship gray above, almost black below the waterline, where the dark mud clung to his massive flanks. Head-on, with scrawny neck extended, upper lip curved like a beak, he reminded me of a huge snapping turtle; here was a true prehistoric monster rising from the swamps of a long lost world.

Though within twenty yards of him, we were in no danger. Rhinos will occasionally charge an elephant, slashing with their razor-sharp teeth rather than using their horn. The rhino, or traditionally the unicorn, is the only animal that will attack an elephant. "But his huge strength nor subtle wit can not / Defend him from the sly Rhinocerot." Fortunately the elephants in Kaziranga are trained to stand firm.

The amazing thing about the Indian rhino is his hide. Heavily folded, studded with rivetlike tubercles, it looks like armor plate, though actually it is easily cut and bleeds readily. The famous Indian naturalist, E. P. Gee, recounts the legend of how the rhino got its armor plating. "Once upon a time Lord Krishna decided to give up elephants as battle animals, and to use the rhino, because mahouts were too easy a target for enemy archers. So a rhino was captured, dressed in armor and trained. But when the animal was brought before Lord Krishna, it was found that it was too stupid to learn and obey orders, so it was driven back to the forest — with its armor still on it." "As a matter of fact," Gee continues, "rhino were actually used by some of the old kings in India as front-line 'tanks' in warfare. They had iron tridents fixed to their horns . . ."

Presently seven rhinos were in sight, dotted around the open grassland. One of them stood mooselike in the shallow water, his face whiskered from a mouthful of aquatic plants. A large heron, reminiscent of our great blue, alighted at the water's edge, near a raft of Brahminy ducks. A flock of long-tailed green parrots flew overhead with raucous shrieks. And now in the distance emerged the perfect background to this dreamlike scene: the long, jagged range of the Himalayas, white towers against a pale-blue sky.

To see the Indian rhino in such a setting is worth a hundred theoretical arguments for wildlife conservation — just as an hour among the redwoods will convince the most practical man that a tree may be worth more alive than dead. The poachers, however, are immune to the conservationists' arguments; to them, a dead rhino can be worth a lifetime's honest wages. Not long ago a rich Indian who fell ill in London sent home for the blood of a freshly killed rhino, just as men in the Middle Ages sought unicorn blood to heal their wounds. Generally, however, rhino blood is not in great demand; most poachers merely saw off the horns and leave the bodies to rot.

During the two years previous to our visit, 24 animals had been killed by poachers. For a slow-breeding species (one calf every three years) this is a dangerous rate of attrition. Only the strictest methods of protection, of both the living animal and its habitat, can save it.

Wherever he still exists, the rhino is at bay. The two African species, provided the native governments maintain the parks and reserves, will undoubtedly win through. In Asia, the Sumatran rhino, which so impressed Marco Polo, has all but disappeared within a single generation, perhaps to join in oblivion the other species of animals that have become extinct, through man's agency. The Javan rhino may endure for a while in the fastness of his remote peninsula. The great Indian, despite continued depredations, has a better than even chance of survival, though his numbers are slowly diminishing.

In a wholly tamed and manicured world there would be no room for the rhinoceros; he would become as much of an anachronism as did the unicorn in the age of reason. Yet to those who need what Henry Thoreau called "the tonic of wildness," the rhino's great horn, not in a powder but firmly planted on his living, breathing nose, is worth more than its weight in gold.

Meanwhile as the rhino becomes scarcer, the actual market price of his horn goes up. His supposed contribution to the art of love has become the greatest threat to his existence. He is battling for life against a legend.

— 10 —

The Conservation
Revolution

D<small>ON'T WORRY</small>, the ecology fad is almost over. It's going to be Women's Liberation next year. Then male counterrevolution the year after. Then something else." In contrast to that remark, which I overheard not long ago, here are three typical statements by persons who have taken a different view:

> "Most people are *on* the world, not in it — have no conscious sympathy or relationship to anything about them — undiffused, separate, and rigidly alone."

> "Of all organic beings, man alone is to be regarded as a destructive power . . . He wields energies to resist which nature is wholly impotent . . . Though living *in* physical nature, he is not *of* her."

> "What is the use of a house if you haven't got a tolerable planet to put it on?"

The sentiments are familiar enough. The interesting thing is the date when they were set down. The first was written by John Muir, perhaps in the 1880s. The second by George Perkins Marsh in 1864. The third by Henry D. Thoreau, in a letter to a friend in 1860. And let me add one more, written by Bernard DeVoto about John Wesley Powell, the first man to run the Grand Canyon a century ago: "His vision was to make the land *live* rather than die, to build a society that may have decent security and dignity in accord with the conditions set by nature."

Such statements — and one could find countless others — suggest that the current interest in man's relation to his environment is not just a passing fad. A groundswell of ecological understanding has been building up for a long time, but groundswells are likely to be ignored until eventually they come crashing down on the beach in a roar of surf. At the moment, the noise is loud enough for anyone to hear. Truths that a few wise men have been preaching for at least a century have suddenly become common knowledge — so much so that it is difficult to write about the ecological revolution in general terms without sounding trite.

One point seems clear: there is nothing to be gained by lumping together everyone in power as "The Establishment," made up of evil men. For example, we can agree with former Senator Gruening on the need for birth control and the wrongness of the Vietnam War and still disagree with him about damming the Yukon River in Alaska. Rather than simply crying out against the so-called Establishment, isn't it more useful to study specific instances of how power may corrupt, how it is exerted, how it can be counteracted? In this connection, I cannot wholly agree with those who inveigh against "piecemeal" actions as almost worse than nothing, who say that what we want is not reform but revolution, that it is futile to clean up rivers and purify exhaust from automobiles when we should be banning all automobiles and challenging the ethics of our society. This is the either / or fallacy. We need both reform *and* revolution. Of course the aims of conservationists are revolutionary — they are radical in the literal sense of that term, since they go to the root of our system of values. But without "piecemeal" reforms in our treatment of the environment, pretty soon a large part of the country will be beyond saving, by revolution or anything else. Yet we read statements like this: "If you believe that thermal pollution will soon raise the oceans by fifty feet (by melting the ice caps), how can you work on enlarging Cape Cod National Seashore? If you believe, as some do, that increasing population will cause us to starve in twenty years, how can you even work on thermal pollution?"

It is also true that so-called piecemeal actions — i.e., dealing with one specific aspect of environmental deterioration — can lead directly to revolution on a broader scale. One obvious example is Rachel Carson and her famous book, *Silent Spring*. Again and again, her name has come up in connection with the environmental revolution. To quote a recent editorial: "It was only eight years ago that Rachel Carson published *Silent Spring* and already it has had an effect comparable with that of the bomb or the population explosion. It goes to show that the printed word, well or beautifully written, still carries impact . . . A few thousand words from her, and the world took a new direction." The story of that book demonstrates what one person can do, dealing with a highly

technical subject, provided that she has the talent and courage and sheer drive to see it through.

I suggested at the beginning that we have now reached the

point where pressures on the environment are greater than
it can tolerate. This is particularly true of our remaining
wilderness. If our present technical means of exploitation

had existed in the nineteenth century, we might well have lost what we now recognize as a national treasure: those few areas of virgin land that remain, like bright spots on a flaking fresco, to remind us of how our country looked before the white man came. A giant redwood that previously took days to cut down with a handsaw can now be felled by modern machinery in a matter of minutes. Where the forty-niners' pick and shovel made a mere scratch on the landscape, dredges now literally eat into the hillsides and excrete sterile gravel to leave behind a permanent wasteland. Copper and other refineries destroy vegetation for tens of miles in every direction from the source of their deadly fumes, open-pit mines create craters large enough to be seen from the moon. At least these forms of destruction are clearly visible and easily understood; we can't help seeing what we are doing. Not quite so blatant, though at last being recognized, is the slow poisoning and downgrading of the entire environment. Eventually, anyone who can read and use his five senses must become aware of what is going on. The question is, what can we do about it?

Big business and government agencies have a ready answer: call in the public-relations boys and persuade the public to take it. When *Silent Spring* was published the National Agricultural Chemicals Association did not attempt to deal with the hazards that the book had exposed. Instead it appropriated a quarter of a million dollars in an attempt to prove — unsuccessfully — that Rachel Carson was a hysterical fool. When cigarette smoking was proved to be a major factor in lung cancer, how did the tobacco industry react? By pretty advertisements that associated cigarette smoking with youth and health and the freshness of the great outdoors. By publicity campaigns that sought to discredit the findings of the research scientists as somehow inconclusive. The approach here is a sort of parody of our criminal code. It assumes that you are an irresponsible alarmist until you can be proved dead. One is reminded of the tests for witchcraft in early New England. Throw the suspect into the pond. If she floats she is a witch, and is promptly hanged; if she sinks she is innocent. But by then it is rather late.

Government agencies also rely on high-level blandishments to smooth the way for doubtful and dangerous projects. As we have seen, when the Atomic Energy Commission wanted to experiment with shallow underground explosions, Edward Teller tried to persuade the people of Alaska that they needed a harbor north of the Arctic Circle. They didn't; the explosions wouldn't have made a usable harbor anyway, as the AEC well knew, while the side effects might well have been disastrous.

Similarly, when the Army Engineers wanted to dam the Yukon River, a high-powered public-relations firm was employed to sell the idea, promising local prosperity through sale of power and somehow transforming a future icebound artificial lake surrounded by mudflats into an ideal summer resort. The pattern keeps repeating itself. We had better brace ourselves for an attempt to "condition" us to accept the unbearable boom of the supersonic transport. The problem of the SST, we are told, is being approached in a truly scientific spirit. Experiments have been conducted by the Army in several major cities to determine how destructive the boom is to property, and how much noise a man can take without quite going nuts. Pregnant rats were also subjected to the boom to see what it does to the unborn embryo. The resulting rise of 400 percent in the mortality of the litter would seem to the layman quite alarming; but the official report, aimed at soothing the public, declared that there was no appreciable effect.

This Madison Avenue approach to public policy is a logical extension of one of the basic myths of our time. "Leave it to the experts," we are told, "they are dealing with technical matters that you can't possibly understand." As Sheldon Novick wrote in *The Careless Atom*, social and political issues that depend on technology "are effectively screened from outside examination by the public's — and in most cases, the Congress's — lack of facts . . . we have been given not information, but judgments propounded by experts." Yet it has been proved again and again that the general public is quite capable of understanding scientific facts if they are properly presented. Of course experts throughout the ages have been aware that they jeopardize their power by giving their secrets to the masses — or even worse by confessing that there *are* no secrets. This axiom is recognized today by the military, by many federal agencies, and by all successful witch doctors. A few centuries ago one risked one's life by translating the Word of God into the vernacular. Today the Word of the Expert carries a similar air of sanctity in our technological society.

For sheer double talk, it is hard to match a self-styled expert who is trying to conceal the facts — or rather the lack of facts — on which he bases his conclusions. And as Barry Commoner reminds us in his book, *Science and Survival*,

"The military hold no monopoly on the imposition of scientific secrecy; industrial competition may have the same result." He quotes the opening paragraph of an article on the toxicology of weed killers, supposedly written by an expert to enlighten the reader and encourage further study. Listen to this: "Many of the toxicological data underlying assessment of the risks involved by using them [weed killers] in practice originate from confidential, non-published reports placed at the disposal of the authorities concerned. Such data have not been included in the present survey."

The myth of the expert — fostered by secrecy, sustained by modern techniques of persuasion — is a priceless asset to any public or private operator who would manipulate the environment and at the same time manipulate people to accept the results of his meddling. The environment can't fight back but fortunately the people can. Individuals and small groups have of course been fighting back for years, but only recently has the "quiet crisis," as Stewart Udall called it, become a full-scale revolution. The modern priesthood of the technician begins to lose its hold on the common people as the latter become scientifically literate and able to judge for themselves. The bones and the feathers that spill from the medicine man's bag turn out to be only bones and feathers after all. One doesn't need a Ph.D. in physics or chemistry to understand that crops can be successfully grown without indiscriminate use of persistent poisons, that technical means exist for controlling smog and for keeping industrial wastes and raw sewage out of our rivers, that the lumber industry can exist and flourish without raiding our remaining virgin forest, that strip mining is not the best way of obtaining coal

— in terms of land use — but only the quickest and the cheapest. In other words, the public knows that we can save the environment if we will. It knows that we have the money, as it reads about the cost of the space program, of a supersonic plane (that would overwhelmingly *increase* noise and other pollution), even of a fabulously expensive and highly questionable federal highway program. These are matters of priority, of choice. To say that we "can't afford" the cost of saving the environment is absurd. It is not an economic but a political decision.

The same people who, only a few years ago, brushed off the conservation movement as a "rear-guard action," now like to dismiss the current concern for ecology as a mere excuse for making trouble. Typical of their thinking is an indignant letter I received not long ago about an article in which I had quoted the comment by Dr. René Dubos that "the most hopeful sign for the future is the attempt by the rebellious youth to reject our social values." The letter read in part: "The fact is that most youth, or adults, who rebel do so against authority in general, and do so only for the sake of rebelling, just as the quote clearly says." This is precisely what Dubos doesn't say. The rebellion is against unacceptable social values which can be defined quite specifically. It is also *for* very specific goals. One of these, in an ever more man-made and industrialized society, is the simple right to enjoy the wild places of the earth.

Wilderness clearly has an impact on man beyond the purely visual. It is coming to be recognized as a part of Western culture, as it has always been in the civilization of the East. To the Chinese painter the natural landscape is a veil through which one may glimpse a loftier reality. Shelley gazed up at Mont Blanc: ". . . I look on high; / Has some unknown omnipotence unfurled / The veil of life and death?" For Emerson, the flowers, the animals, the mountains reflected the wisdom of his best hour. In the presence of nature a "wild delight" runs through him: "I am glad to the brink of fear."

The spiritual values of wilderness gain strength as man becomes more urbanized. When so much of our entertainment, of our intellectual and emotional stimulation, reaches us at second hand, we welcome the chance to make our own response: humility, perhaps, as we stare down the stratified walls of a canyon and see man's tiny place in the scale of time; loneliness, as we lie out in the desert under the stars; surprise, as we come upon a hidden mountain lake or meet a wide-antlered elk at the turn of the trail; terror, almost, when we hear the roar of a flash flood or watch storm waves lashing a rocky coast. We sense the sheer drive of life in the salmon leaping the falls, its exuberance in the short summer burst of alpine flowers at snowline or in the bloom of the desert after rain. We see the beauty of the transitory as we become aware of the cycle of the day and the cycle of the year. Wilderness is as essential to our way of life as our laboratories, museums, libraries. For our need to understand the world of nature signifies something in us deeper than mere curiosity. Here, we feel, is some statement of the truth, if only we have the wisdom to read it.

Postscript to Chapter 7

As this book goes to press, word comes that the Oklawaha River has been saved. On January 19, 1971, President Nixon ordered a halt to further construction of the Cross-Florida Barge Canal "to prevent potentially serious environmental damage."

Photographs:
Identifications
and Credits